Discerning Of Spirits

Seven Dimensions of Revelation

Demontae A. Edmonds

Rejoice Essential Publishing
P.O. BOX 512
Effingham, SC 29541
www.republishing.org

Unless otherwise indicated, scripture is taken from the King James Version

Author's website:www.F4Nations.com

Discerning Of Spirits/Demontae A. Edmonds

ISBN-10: 1-946756-40-7

ISBN-13: 978-1-946756-40-4
Library of Congress Control Number: 2018957727

Dedication

This book is dedicated to the new breed of believers and ministers of the Gospel that God is raising up to reap the End Time Harvest of souls; and also, to the many unsung heroes in third-world nations who share the Gospel in the face of tremendous persecution!

Endorsements

I have been ministering in the areas of inner healing and deliverance for more than forty years. Apostle Edmonds' book teaches new, fresh and vitally important concepts for those who are anointed by God to set the captives free. He shares a heartfelt objective for the reader to gain a deeper understanding of the revelatory dimensions of the Holy Spirit. Clearly, he has met his objective.

Both a novice as well as a seasoned believer used in deliverance ministry will glean fresh nuggets of biblical truth and practical application. Transparency is the hallmark of Apostle Edmonds' writing. Edmonds is not afraid to open the doors of his experiences as a learner, teacher and a servant.

Discerning of Spirits:7 Dimensions Of Revelation will be the next 'go to' book for those who desire to grow deeper in their knowledge and practical application of the dimensions of the Holy Spirit. I will include this book in my core curriculum of mandatory reading for training individuals and teams in inner healing and deliverance ministry."

Dr. Peggy Elliott
Adviser to President Bill Clinton on Race Relations &
Affirmative Action
Peggy Elliott Ministries, St Paul, Minnesota
Author of "Understanding and Breaking Free From Generational Curses" and "I'm Finally Free"

***

"In Apostle Edmond's new book *Discerning of Spirits: 7 Dimensions of Revelation* he dives deep into this subject and opens up our understanding of what this gift entails. In this book you'll hear biblically-based balanced teaching on discernment. You'll read riveting testimonies of experiences with the Lord Jesus Christ and the realms of glory. And my favorite; you'll also receive true wisdom from a seasoned discerner who will teach you how to steward this gift and apply it in your life and ministry. Have your highlighters ready and be prepared to take notes! This is a rich reservoir of revelation which is sure to take your spiritual life to another level!"

Rev. Stephen Powell
Founder & President
Lion of Light Ministries
Fort Mills, SC

***

"In today's society, there are not many with a true father's heart for the people of God. Apostle Demontae Edmonds demonstrates his love for God's people as he shares personal revelation of the realm of the Spirit. The gifts of the Spirit are critical in the times when people are losing hope. Counterfeit voices and ungodly choices are flooding the Body of Christ. In His book, *Discerning of Spirits: 7 Dimensions of Revelation*, unlocks and makes accessible realms of the Spirit which only few have entered.

The reader is able to carefully discern the counterfeit by studying the genuine. Apostle Edmonds trail blazes a path from the heart of

God opening a gateway for believers to receive from heaven. The inner workings of the soul and spirit are unveiled in a skillful, yet practical way which prompts the heart to desire more of God. As one journeys through his testimonies of encounters with the Spirit, faith is released allowing the believer to gain understanding and wisdom to operate in the authentic gift of discerning of Spirits. The Spirit of the Lord is using Apostle Demontae as a weapon, in these end times, to destroy the works of the enemy by ushering the believer into new realms of faith and expectancy, birthing a new breed of spiritual warriors who work miracles. This is a book will not only enrich your spiritual life but it is an enjoyable read."

Dr. Kim Y.Black
Dominion Ministries International, Hampton, VA
ROAR *Institute*
Author of "The Visible Kingdom"

***

"It was a joy reading in print the wisdom that was already stirring in the heart of the author. I have heard Apostle Edmonds speak several times and I could hear his voice as I was reading each word. From beginning to end, one can sense the Spirit of God desiring to fill the heart of the believer/reader with truth and light. Revelation is an essential key for growth. Once we learn something we have an opportunity to flourish. *Discerning of Spirits: 7 Dimensions of Revelation* is a perfect read for those of us who are interested in expanding our spiritual life."

Tanya-Gould Street
U.S. Advisory Council on Human Trafficking
Founder of Identifiable Me

***

"Demontae Edmonds has pressed a good button here. So many people have tripped up because they did not properly discern in the Spirit what was happening around them. Finding out later is often too late to rectify the lost opportunities or damages for the individuals involved. Read this book, learn from it and be an effective minister of deliverance. Helping to set people free is an awe-some experience for your ministry and *Discerning Spirits:7 Dimensions of Revelation* is a resource, which will aid in your pursuits!"

Kathie Walters
Kathie Walters Ministries
Macon, GA

***

Contents

Acknowledgments

This book is dedicated to my wife Jessica Edmonds who has supported and co-labored with me throughout the years in ministry, and has shown unflinching willingness to allot me time to complete the writing of this book. Special appreciation is given to those who have encouraged me continually over the years: My family, Prophet Reggie, the Maples, Prophetess Treena, Elder Jackie, Christina Silina, Shannon Williams, Sylvia, Alana Brown, Apostle Sammie & Dr. Kim Black, and many others.

Foreword

"There is nothing quite like living a life directed by the Holy Spirit.

Romans 8:14 "For as many as are led by the Spirit of God, they are the sons of God."

We were not created to only hear from God occasionally. This is a lie that has been masterfully sold to God's people by the enemy. Our promise is divine guidance. We have an internal compass that never lets us down, but we have to learn to live tuned in!

The prophetic realm is the realm of revelation. It is not for spiritual supermen or women but for every born-again child of God. God's guidance and the potential of your own human spirit to be directed by The Master are life-changing. Every time you stepped out and fell flat on your face, you missed it somewhere! I know it is painful and embarrassing, but it also teaches you. Don't miss out on the teachable moment that God is trying to have with you. Missing it can teach you as much as hitting it on target. Prophetic people have to be surrendered, humble, and quick learners!

One of the most remarkable gifts ever given is the discerning of spirits. It is the ability to peel back the curtain and see accurately into the realm of the spirit. It will save you years of trouble, providing clear answers. It is also a gift that is easy to overlook if you do not learn all of the ways it can function. There are depths and realms of this gift that you have most likely overlooked or are completely unaware of. Not only that, but the enemy has intentionally blocked you from the portion of revelation that is assigned to you.

This writing from Demontae Edmonds will shut down the voice of the enemy and supercharge your spirit man to function in the prophetic realm. This book is a vital weapon in your arsenal. As you turn the pages, you will go from revelation to revelation and instruction to instruction. Demontae not only teaches but shares practical experiences that drive the point home. This book is a must read for every prophetic person.

Understand that God has never lost a battle and Satan has never outwitted our Father! With this in mind, we need to rise to a higher level of sight and sound in the realm of the spirit and quit permitting the thoughts of defeat and bondage. We have been made to see and hear! It is time. Get your highlighter ready, or your finger if you are on a device, and dive deep into the pages of this stunning book. You are exiting the era of stumbling in the dark and entering a lifestyle of illumination."

Ryan LeStrange
Founder TRIBE Network & Ryan LeStrange Ministries
Author:Hell's Toxic Trio

Discerning Of Spirirts

Dimensions Of Revelation

Introduction

Much of the teaching in this book, "*Discerning of Spirits: Seven Dimensions of Revelation,*" was gained from a direct visitation from the Lord Jesus Christ. This visitation will be shared later within the book. As you read this book, you will gain a greater knowledge and insight of some of the inner workings of the Kingdom of God and realm of the spirit.

The gifts of the Holy Spirit are part of our divine inheritance as believers. They can serve as powerful weapons in the hands of believers to destroy the works of darkness. Also, they can be used for the edification and building up of the Kingdom of God on the earth. In this present hour, there is a great resurgence of interest in the gifts of the Spirit as believers are desirous to walk in the supernatural power of God.

In this book, one specific and powerful gift of the Spirit will be discussed. The gift of discerning of spirits is one of the most valued yet misunderstood of the nine gifts. It is a multi-dimensional gift that can allow us revelatory access into the hidden realms of the spirit. The invisible realm becomes visible when this gift is in operation.

Isaiah 8:18-19 says, "Behold, I and the children whom the Lord hath given me are for signs and for wonders in Israel from the Lord of hosts, which dwelleth in mount Zion. And when they shall say unto you, seek unto them that have familiar spirits, and unto wizards that peep, and that mutter: should not a people seek unto their God? for the living to the dead?" Psychic hotlines, television shows with mediums, and professional magicians have become popular in our modern age due to the interest in the supernatural. Satan is only able to counterfeit God's true creation and intention.

God is raising up believers who will authentically operate in the supernatural through the

Holy Spirit. Understanding the gift of discerning of spirits is vital to exposing the counterfeit works of darkness. As you read this book, rise up as God's son or daughter who was made for signs and wonders!

CHAPTER 1

Jesus Visits With A Rebuke

THAT SCARY CHURCH SERVICE

I grew up attending traditional Southern Baptist churches. The messages of salvation, water baptism, repentance, forgiveness, and communion were routinely preached. Most of the messages centered on Jesus and there was little mention of the Holy Spirit and His ministry. The God of the Bible could hear us, see us, and answer our prayers, but never did I hear anyone mention hearing from God directly. As a youth, I read in the Bible how God spoke to men and women of old and used them to do great acts. I had a hunger to be one of those people, but it seemed unattainable.

One Sunday morning, I was sitting in a church service with my friend George. We both were 17 years old and decided to go to a local Baptist church in our town. At the end of the sermon, the pastor said the most unusual thing, "God just spoke to me!" How audacious and peculiar for a preacher, let alone anyone, to say publicly that God spoke to them. The speaker was a well-respected minister that God had sent from New York to Virginia to pastor. I listened in expectation waiting to see what he would say next.

"God spoke to me. There is an elderly woman here in this church. You have been in church your entire life, but you have never truly given your heart to Jesus Christ. You have a lot of bitterness in your heart. This is your last call. You are knocking on death's door. If you don't receive Jesus this time, there will not be another opportunity!" My friend George and I looked at each other in disbelief and awe. This was totally out of the norm for what we were used to in church services. At that exact moment, the lights flickered and temporarily went out in the church. We looked at each other again with a stare communicating the thought that we both now were thinking, "This is God!"

An elderly woman came up to the altar and confessed she had been in church her entire life but never truly accepted Jesus as her Lord. She gave her life to the Lord and repented of her sins. Many others were saved that day. We felt the fear of God grip our souls. After leaving the church, we discussed how "scary," "spooky," and "real" this occurrence was to us. We didn't understand all of what just happened, but we knew it was God. We felt like the people witnessing Jesus' ministry in action. Luke 5:26 states, "And they were all amazed, and they glorified God, and were filled with fear, saying, we have seen strange things today!"

GROWING IN THE HOLY SPIRIT

This was my first public experience with one of the gifts of the Spirit and the prophetic ministry in operation. The terms "prophetic" and "gifts of the Spirit" were not in my vocabulary at the time. I had never heard them taught, referenced, and certainly never saw them demonstrated. This would be one of the early incidents that God would use to give me a hunger and zeal to understand the Holy Spirit and deeper things of God.

In my early 20s, I began to attend a Pentecostal church. For the first time, I heard people speak in tongues, prophesy, and interpret tongues. People would testify of healings taking place by the power of God. I would watch as individuals got delivered from demonic oppressions and bondages. It was all new, fresh, and exciting to learn and watch the Holy Spirit at work. Fellowshipping with this ministry and another local ministry caused me to grow even more in my knowledge of God and spiritual things. Soon enough, I too would be hearing the voice of the Holy Spirit and being used by Him to bless people's lives.

Many manifestations that were new to my Christian experience would happen. Seasoned leaders would help me to understand what was taking place in my life. Some of these things would unnerve me and I would have to seek God directly for answers. He would always send someone to speak prophetically to me or give me insight by His Word and Holy Spirit. God took me through a seven-year "wilderness season" where natural things (finances, career, and relationships) seemed to dry up, but the things of the Spirit became more evident and real.

Almost as soon as I surrendered to the Lord, He began to use me powerfully by His Spirit. Prophetic gifts, healing, and deliverance began to flow from my life. Wonderful testimonies were being shared by those that God led me to minister to. The more God used me, the more I wanted to not only be used but understand the depths and intricacies of the things of God. God launched me into pastoring and I began to teach from years of training, practice, study, and walking with God.

TEACHING THE NATIONS

When I pastored a church, the power of God increased, the gifts became sharper and pronounced, and the supernatural was more commonplace. Others in the Christian community viewed our ministry as the "supernatural church," "place to go for healing" or "the church with the miracles!" Others began to encourage me to share my teachings through videos and CD. One of the videos that I recorded is still up today. It is entitled "Discerning of Spirits" on YouTube: https://www.youtube.com/watch?v=fq07Ch9_d04

In the YouTube video, I shared a short teaching on the gift of discerning of spirits. I discussed its purpose, function, and availability to believers. Specifically, I shared in the video how the gift operated within four realms or dimensions. At the end of the video, there is a real life powerful demonstration of the gift in action to bring deliverance to a young lady by the power of God. At that time, this video was heralded as one of our best teaching videos and there was great feedback.

As the ministry expanded, God opened up doors for me to travel across the United States, Asia, Europe, and Africa to share the Gospel. God allowed me to teach and instruct pastors and churches around the world. Many times, I taught on the topic of the gift of discerning of spirits in different nations. I would teach much of the same message that I shared in previous meetings and from the video teaching that our ministry posted on YouTube.

As miracles, signs, and wonders multiplied in our ministry, the demand for teaching on the things of the Spirit also increased. Many began to regard me as an expert in the gifts of the Spirit and supernatural realm of God. Soon I would have a personal encounter with the real expert and master teacher! No matter how much you have done or seen in life or ministry, God always desires to bring us into greater "present truth." 2 Peter 1:12 says, "Wherefore I will not be negligent to put you always in remembrance of these things, though ye know them, and be established in the present truth."

"YOU ARE NOT TEACHING IT RIGHT!"

As ministers of the Gospel, one can preach on a topic for years. After careful study, hearing other ministers, and research, we can often feel that our teaching on a topic is comprehensive or accurate. It takes the Spirit of God to illuminate new truths and breathe life into the Word of God to give us new insights. This happened to a man of God named Martin Luther when God enlightened him on the scripture, "*The just shall live by faith* (Hebrews 10:38)." This one revelation and the insights tied to it would be the catalyst for him nailing his 95 Theses on Castle Church in Wittenberg. This was one of the events that thrusted Europe into the Protestant Reformation. If we are open to be taught, then God is always willing to teach us new things.

One night, after teaching on various topics including discerning of spirits, the Lord appeared to me in a dream. The dream was actually a night vision similar to the one that the prophet Daniel had in Daniel 7:2, "Daniel spoke and said, I saw in my vision by night and behold." In the vision, the Lord Jesus descended from heaven out of the sky and appeared to me. He hovered about 10 feet over me in the air and spoke with a loud authoritative voice, "You have been faithful to teach My Word, but you have not taught accurately on the gift of discerning of spirits. You have taught that this gift operates in four different dimensions. I have come to show you that you are wrong! It operates in seven. I will show you in My Word the other three dimensions that you do not include within your teachings."

The night vision was short in length but lasting in its impact upon my soul. Jesus spoke very few words from His mouth, and part of the vision He spoke from His Spirit to my spirit. He wasted no words in sharing with me the message that He was released to share. Although I had taught the topic of discerning of spirits half accurately, He did not seem upset or mad. Jesus was appearing to set the record straight and honor my sincerity to preach the Word.

My spirit man was alive and awakened by the appearance of Jesus Christ in this vision. Jesus had appeared to me several times previously through dreams and visions. All of the visitations except one were unexpected. As He spoke, "I will explain to you the other three that you do not include within your teachings," instantly a divine download of revelation and insight poured into my spirit from the Spirit of God. Scriptures and insight in regard to the fullness of the teaching on the gift of discerning of spirits flooded me.

In this book, I'm going to share from the experience and teaching that God gave me through years of ministry, practice, and study. In addition, I will share on the three additional dimensions that the gift of discerning of spirits operates in to give us revelation and insight. You too will grasp the full teaching on the topic as I understand it at this time. It is my sincere prayer that as you read this book, the Holy Spirit will "open the eyes of your understanding" (Ephesians 1:18), give new access into the realm of the Spirit and a new appreciation for the dynamic giftings Jesus paid for with the sacrifice of His own life.

CHAPTER 2

Discerning the Angelic Dimension

Since time immemorial, mankind has been fascinated with angels. Throughout history and ancient times, there have been records and accounts of angelic-like beings. These angelic beings were often benevolent and interested in the affairs of humans. From Genesis to Revelations, one can read about angels and their ministry to mankind. In the Bible, we find angels assisting Abraham, destroying the cities of Sodom and Gomorrah, leading the children of Israel out of Egypt, wrestling with Jacob, relaying a message to people at Jesus' resurrection, and serving as part of God's end-time army returning with Christ.

In modern times, angels have continued to capture the attention of mankind. There have been numerous books written about angels. Some of these books have been written by individuals who had near-death experiences where angels intervened to save their life. The popular television show *Touched by An Angel* that aired for nine years and 211 episodes, has helped to increase the allure of angels. Another popular television show, *Unsolved Mysteries,* broadcasted a number of episodes involving personal testimonies of people who encountered angelic beings.

The gift of discerning of spirits (1 Corinthians 12:10) at times allows us to see into the realm of angels and angelic activities. This is one of the seven dimensions that this gift may operate within. This dimension of the gift is often strong with seer prophets and high-ranking intercessors. It is a privilege and honor when the Holy Spirit endows us to discern these supernatural beings. When God opens our senses to discern these dynamic beings, it is always to make known part of His divine will and eternal purposes.

SENSING ANGELS!

One may discern angels or angelic activity without seeing or hearing them. The most common way that people discern angels is through sensing their presence. In my own ministry, I have declared to the audience, "The angel of God is here!" It doesn't always mean that I have seen the angel, but I will suddenly feel a person standing beside or near me where no human is present. Many times, I will feel an angelic presence stand near my right or left side while ministering. When this happens, the prophetic gifting will become heightened and prophetic words will become more detailed, precise, and accurate.

Once I prophesied to a fellow minister, "I see two angels assigned to your ministry. One is named Miracles and other is named Revelation. I see in a vision that they stand by your side in big meetings." He confirmed that the prophetic word was accurate. Later that day, this man of God showed me an old photo of him ministering at a large crusade years ago. In the photo, I could clearly see the outline of two opaque silhouettes in the shapes of men standing to his right and left. He explained that, in this crusade and as well as others, whenever he sensed the presence of these two angels, miracles and salvations would be at an explosive level. He had seen the blind see, deaf hear, dead raised, and lame walk while preaching to crowds that numbered up to 250,000.

Acts 2:1-2 says, "And when the day of Pentecost was fully come, they were all with one accord in one place. And suddenly there came a sound from heaven as of a rushing mighty wind, and it filled all the house where they were sitting." I believe that when the Holy Spirit was poured out upon the early disciples, the sound of the mighty rushing wind was not only the Holy Spirit but also angelic reinforcements being released from heaven to earth. The church at Jerusalem multiplied exponentially after this outpouring. Thousands were added to the church in a single day.

There are times that the Holy Spirit may allow us to discern a manifestation as a sign of angelic presence. Years ago, when I pastored, a message through tongues and interpretation was released to the congregation. Part of the prophetic message was that God was going to release new angels to the ministry and that the church would experience a surge of the supernatural. Near the end of the prophetic utterance, we all felt a strong gust of wind blow through the building. It brought with it a wave of repentance and intercession. We were allowed to discern the wave of angels just prophesied about being released as prophetic fulfillment. Many screamed and cried out at the presence of these mighty angels that manifested like wind. Hebrews 1:7 NLT states, "He sends his angels like winds."

Angels carry a great degree of the presence of Heaven. Wherever they are present, the atmosphere in the room changes. In meetings, what I call a "holy hush" may come over the service and people present. People stop moving, and no longer walk around; a sense of reverence fills the air; and even babies stop crying. This holy hush happens when angelic forces arrive on the scene bringing with them the fear of God. Although most may not see the angels present, they will certainly sense them. The holy fear that these angels carry have caused many to be afraid at their divine appearance. In the Bible, angels' most common greeting is, "Fear Not!" (Daniel 10:12; Luke 1:13; Genesis 21:17; Luke 2:10; Matthew 28:5).

HEARING ANGELS!

When the gift of discerning of spirits is in operation, the Holy Spirit may open someone's spiritual ears to hear into the angelic realm. One should not seek to hear angels as it may open the door for deception. We should be open to hearing from heaven as the Holy Spirit leads. God's primary means of communicating with us is through the Word and Spirit of God. There are circumstances and special situations that God may allow us to hear or discern angels speaking to us.

In 2005, I was in a prayer service when I saw two gentlemen walk into the room. To my left, I heard an audible voice say about one of the men, "He is a great prophet!" I looked at the man and honestly, he didn't look like a great anything. He grabbed the microphone and began to prophesy to me, "I see an angel standing beside the left of you. He is bent over and whispering into your left ear. This angel is helping to bring an increase of the word of wisdom in your life and ministry." I was blown away! Just moments before, I heard the angel audibly and now the prophet was prophesying what only God could reveal. Since that encounter, we remain good friends. God allowed him to discern into the angelic realm.

Hagar and her young son Ishmael were in a desperate situation wandering in the wilderness of Beersheba. They had little food, in a hot dry climate, vulnerable to attackers, and having no place to go. The bottle of water they shared together was now empty. Walking through a desert or wilderness with no water can cause one to fall unconscious or die from dehydration. Genesis 21:17-19 reveals, "And God heard the voice of the lad; and the angel of God called to Hagar out of heaven, and said unto her, What aileth thee, Hagar? fear not; for God hath heard the voice of the lad where he is. Arise, lift up the lad, and hold him in thine hand; for I will make him a great nation. And God opened her eyes, and she saw a well of water; and she went, and filled the bottle with water, and gave the lad drink." In these verses, Hagar only heard the voice without seeing the angel.

SEEING ANGELS!

Seeing an angel is an experience one never forgets. The experience can be frightening, exciting, and overwhelming all at once. Sensing or hearing an angel is supernatural, but seeing an angel takes on another level of intensity. There have been thousands of individuals around the globe who have attested to seeing these awesome beings. Many books and short stories have been written from these accounts.

Angels may be seen in diverse ways. One may see an angel in a dream. Joseph saw angels in dreams that instructed him when to take his family to Egypt, and when to return from Egypt (Matthew 2:13). An angel may appear within an inner or closed vision. This type of vision is one that you see in your mind's eye and not externally. They may also appear in an open vision like the one I saw standing beside my bed with the sword. Paul saw an angel in an open vision while prisoner aboard a ship headed for Roman. Acts 27:23-24 says, "For there stood by me this night the angel of God, whose I am, and whom I serve Saying, Fear not, Paul; thou must be brought before Caesar: and, lo, God hath given thee all them that sail with thee."

My armor bearer was praying with a group of people for a young lady to be set free by the power of Jesus from emotional bondages. She had suffered some recent traumas in life and was emotionally distraught. As the group prayed, suddenly his spiritual eyes were opened, and he saw an angel dressed in white wielding a sword. The angel cut the spiritual chains wrapped around the lady off and they instantly fell to the ground in the spirit realm. This was his first time seeing an angel and he was so caught off guard by this vision that he didn't share it with the group until later.

Many falsely believe that angels always appear as half-naked beings with large wings. Angels may take on different forms, shapes, or appearances depending on their activity and function. The Holy Spirit may allow you to discern their presence and operation, but not their true spirit form. For instance, some have seen angels as flashes of light, blue flying orbs, orange flying orbs, or even tongues of fire (Acts 2:3). Also, depending on their heavenly rank and function, they may appear taller, shorter, stronger, with wings, without wings, or with fierce countenances.

In a dream, I saw a huge angel that was standing by me decreeing the word of the living God over my life. As he spoke in the dream, he had a huge broadsword planted into the ground. When I awoke from the dream, I saw the exact same angel from the dream in an open vision standing beside my bed with the same sword. When I looked at him, he suddenly turned into a huge ball of glowing orange light and vanished. For hours after this encounter, I felt consumed by the presence of God.

CORPORATE GIFTING

I have been in services where God allowed the gift of discerning of spirits to function in a corporate manner. In 2006, at the Founders Inn in Virginia Beach, I was on the front row during a Catch the Fire ministry conference. Before the meeting, I had prayed one hour for God to bless people during the service. My expectation level was high, but I never imagined what would happen next.

As the worship intensified, I heard an unusual sound that caused my ears to perk up. What was this that I was hearing? I heard an angelic chorus singing above our heads. It sounded like the voice of over a hundred angels but at the same time the voice of one person. The angelic worship was in perfect pitch, tone, harmony, and unity. Wow! My next thought was, "Is anyone else hearing what I'm hearing?" I looked to my left and

I saw Gordon Robertson (current president of CBN) and to my right Dr. Craig Von Buseck both go down to their knees in worship. Many others laid prostrate or worshipped from their knees as many reported that their spiritual ears were open as well to hear the angels sing.

A similar event happened during the birth of Christ. Luke 2:8-14 says, "And there were in the same country shepherds abiding in the field, keeping watch over their flock by night. And, lo, the angel of the Lord came upon them, and the glory of the Lord shone round about them: and they were sore afraid. And the angel said unto them, Fear not: for, behold, I bring you good tidings of great joy, which shall be to all people. For unto you is born this day in the city of David a Savior, which is Christ the Lord. And this shall be a sign unto you; Ye shall find the babe wrapped in swaddling clothes, lying in a manger. And suddenly there was with the angel a multitude of the heavenly host praising God, and saying, Glory to God in the highest, and on earth peace, good will toward men." The shepherds heard a company of angels praising God as the Spirit of God allowed them to discern the angelic chorus.

CONCLUSION

Angels are awe-inspiring but ultimately, they are servants of God. They are God's heavenly ministers and messengers that accomplish His purposes. Hebrews 1:14 proclaims, "Are they not all ministering spirits, sent forth to minister for them who shall be heirs of salvation?" Another word for *minister* is servant. Who are the "heirs of salvation?" Those who have believed on the Lord Jesus Christ and confessed Him as their Savior are heirs of the Kingdom of God. Angels are constantly on assignment working to bring breakthrough, deliverance, healing, salvation, restoration, provision, protection, and answer to prayers for God's children. Also, they work with the Holy Spirit to bring non-believers into the knowledge of Jesus Christ.

In this chapter, I must issue a disclaimer as regards seeing or experiencing angelic activity. These experiences are given by God for specific assignments and to reveal God's will. They are never given to cause pride or fanaticism. Due to the supernatural nature of angels and the awe that they inspire, immature people who see them are often prey to fanaticism. Also, there is a tendency for some with the ability to see these beings to get caught up in pride. Most importantly, the Bible warns us against worshipping angels or any beings. Colossians 2:18 says, "Let no man beguile you of your reward in a voluntary humility and worshipping of angels, intruding into those things which he hath not seen, vainly puffed up by his fleshly mind."

In the Book of Revelation, the Apostle John is caught up into the heaven. In Revelation 19, he encounters a being that he believes to be an angel. John shares with us his response to this being in Revelation 19:10, "And I fell at his feet to worship him." The being rebukes John for his actions and explains that he is not an angel but a fellow servant. He was probably one of the great prophets of old assigned to reveal things to the Apostle John during his heavenly experience. In his glorified body, this servant of God would have seemed like an angel. "*I am thy fellow servant, and of thy brethren that have the testimony of Jesus: worship God: for the testimony of Jesus is the spirit of prophecy.*" John is instructed to only worship God. Any prophetic gift, grace, or experience should ultimately invoke a greater adoration, appreciation, and worship of Jesus Christ.

CHAPTER 3

Discerning Demonic Spirits

The gift of discerning of spirits has seven dimensions that may operate as the Spirit wills. Each of these dimensions allows believers access and revelation into the realm of spirits. The dimension most commonly acquainted with this gifting is the ability to discern demonic activity. Any serious deliverance minister should pray to have this gift in operation in their life and ministry.

Many afflictions in life are the result of demonic infiltration or infestation. Doors opened through sin, disobedience, or general curses can be exploited by demonic spirits. Counseling, self-help books, and generalized prayers may be ineffective if there is a demon present in the life of a person. The antidote is for the person to submit to God, receive deliverance, and live a life according to the Word of God. How can one cast out a demon from an individual without first being aware that it is there? The gift of discerning of spirits gives strategic insight that helps us to know if negative issues in a person's life stems from a natural condition or spiritual attack.

TYPES AND FUNCTIONS

When Jesus delivered an individual, He often identified the type of spirit present. He would say, "Come out thou deaf and dumb spirit" or "Come out of the man you unclean spirit!" When doing deliverance, it is important to be able not only to discern if a spirit is present but also to know the function of that spirit. The function of the spirit or its 'type' will reveal its ability and modus operandi. For example, an unclean spirit may cause a person to neglect their hygiene and engage in fornication. A spirit of fear may have a person consumed by worry, fear, and anxiety. In Mark 9:25, it was revealed that the "deaf and dumb spirit" was behind the suffering of seizures and torment of a little boy.

I remember an experience I once had in this area while conducting a meeting. The anointing was heavy upon me as I laid hands upon people to receive healing in a prayer line. One after another, people fell under the power of God as the Holy Spirit was moving on them for healing. I reached one lady and asked her, "What is your ailment?" She said, "My stomach always hurts, and I have difficulty digesting food." I prayed with her in the same manner that I had prayed for others and she just glanced at me as if she felt nothing.

Again, I prayed and noticed the anointing was not connected with her spirit. Internally, I asked God, "What's happening?" At that moment, my spiritual eyes opened, and I saw a small demon lodged in the middle of the woman's stomach. This miniscule spirit was a spirit of anxiety that caused her health problem. This woman was set free instantly after changing my prayer from one of healing to one of deliverance. The gift of discerning of spirits gave me the strategic edge to gain the victory over Satan in this one's life.

These testimonies serve as examples that identifying the type of spirit functioning behind a demonic activity is important to defeating the enemy. There are times in deliverance that even more information is needed to break the power of the enemy over the life of a person or family. The name or entry point of the spirit may need to be properly discerned. Jesus discovered the name of one spirit as "Legion" because there were many spirits present in a man.

Also, discerning the number of spirits present may be needed for a complete deliverance. I have seen individuals return to the altar multiple times at different meetings to get deliverance again and again. These people often become frustrated because they feel they are not being totally set free. The issue may be that there are multiple demons at work and the number of them needs to be discerned so that all are cast out at once. Luke 8:2 says, "And certain women, which had been healed of evil spirits and infirmities, Mary called Magdalene, out of whom went seven devils." The Bible tells us here that the number of demons cast out of one of Jesus' disciples was known unto them at the point of deliverance.

Another type of spirit that needs to be discerned is the strongman. The strongman is the controlling spirit that is in charge when multiple spirits are attached to a person's life. The strongman is often the root spirits that first open the doors of demonic access to the individual. Casting out the peripheral spirits without dealing with the strongman is like cutting down tree branches but not the tree trunk. When you destroy the strongman's power and authority within the individual's life, it is like putting the axe to the root. Rejection and bitterness are two of the most common strongman spirits.

The strongman spirit serves as both guardian and leader over an individual that is demonically oppressed. Demonic spirits consider people their property or "house" that they live in and control. Mark 3:27 states, "No man can enter into a strong man's house, and spoil his goods, except he will first bind the strong man; and then he will spoil his house." The Bible likens deliverance to the action of robbing a house. If you want to rob the house (i.e. see the captive set free), then first bind up the strong man. The lesser demonic powers are enabled and empowered by the strongman. When his rule is broken, then it is easier to cast them out and set the captive free.

DEMONIC WEAPONS

Many times, in spiritual warfare, I have seen spiritual weapons used by the enemy to attack people. These are often darts, arrows, or knives launched in the spirit realm. Sometimes the demon may not be present, but the effects of these weapons still negatively impact the person's life. There is a video that we have on our YouTube page, which has many awestruck after viewing. In the video, I tell a young lady that she has dealt with betrayal after betrayal. A spirit of betrayal was assigned against her that didn't possess her, but it left a huge spiritual knife in her back. As a prophetic gesture and symbolic act, I pull the knife out of her back without touching and she instantly falls backward under the power of God.

Another time, I was praying for a man and through discerning of spirits, I saw small darts lodged into his chest. I asked him, "Have you been having chest pains?" He said, "Yes. They started not long ago and I'm going to the doctor to get checked out." I told him, "Don't waste your time! I saw small darts in the spirit lodged into your chest. These are word curses spoken against you that must be broken!" He had offended some people within his ministry and they had spoken emotionally charged ill words against him. Demonic spirits empowered these words as small darts to cause him physical pain. The word curses were broken, and the pain went away within one day.

Psalms 64:1-4 says, "Hear my voice, O God, in my prayer: preserve my life from fear of the enemy. Hide me from the secret counsel of the wicked; from the insurrection of the workers of iniquity: Who whet their tongue like a sword, and bend their bows to shoot their arrows, even bitter words: That they may shoot in secret at the perfect: suddenly do they shoot at him, and fear not." The Holy Spirit inspired the words within this psalm written by King David. Notice the language used to describe how enemies may attack us. Bitter words spoken against others are described as arrows. When words are spoken in love and faith, the Spirit of God can energize them to bring life. When words are spoken out of deep hurt, anger, or bitterness, demonic spirits can energize them to bring death and decay. Words can become weapons!

DEVELOPING SPIRITUAL SENSES

The Holy Spirit abides within our human spirit when we are born again. That is why Jesus said in John 7:38, "out of your belly shall flow rivers of living water." When we receive the baptism of the Holy Spirit, our spirits become endued with God's graces in a greater measure. As we grow in the Word and prayer, our spirits become more active and sensitive to the Spirit of God. This spiritual growth can affect how the Holy Spirit releases revelation to our spirit man.

Our spirit has a spiritual body that possesses spiritual senses. Many who have had outer-body experiences or near-death experiences have reported being separated from their natural bodies but still having a spiritual body. This spirit body was the "real them" that could still hear, see, think, smell, and sense. Ecclesiastes 12:7 states, "The spirit shall return unto God who gave it." The Holy Spirit can use any of our five senses to give us discernment.

SENSE OF SMELL

Once during an altar call, I walked past a young man and smelled what I likened unto the smell of skunk. It was a putrid smell that almost made me sick to my stomach. Instantly, I discerned it was an unclean spirit and a spirit of perversion operating together. These two spirits caused the young man to engage in bizarre and abnormal sexual activity. He lived an unclean and perverse lifestyle. One would classify such person as a pervert! This is just one example of how God can use your sense of smell in discernment.

SENSE OF HEARING

"Who said that?" is what I asked myself when praying for a young lady in a church service. While praying for her, a deep guttural voice spoke, "Don't listen to him! Don't believe what he is saying!" I knew it was not the young lady speaking. The voice was an angry man's voice. Also, her mouth had not moved as she stood with her hands uplifted. No one present in the meeting heard the demonic voice, because the words were not spoken out into the physical realm for the natural ears to hear. I realized that my spiritual ears were being opened to discern what the demon was speaking to her. God had me to tell her the exact words the demon was speaking to her mind. She thought it was her own thoughts until this revelation was released. God used this revelation to bring her repentance and bring deliverance to her soul.

In Luke 8, Jesus encounters a demon-possessed man who is called the "Gaderene demoniac." This man was untamable and unstoppable. He was always naked and living in the tombs and wilderness. Luke tells us that the people of that day could not bind him with chains or cuffs. He was a terror to behold! The man energized by the devil confronted Jesus and His ministry team. Luke 8:30 says, "And Jesus asked him, saying, what is thy name? And he said, Legion: because many devils were entered into him." A demonic spirit present recognized Jesus' authority and responded to His inquiry. Jesus' spiritual ears were opened to hear this spirit reveal the name of "Legion."

In this chapter, Jesus' spiritual ears opened even the more and the gift of discerning of spirits increased upon His life. Luke 8:31 says, "And they besought him that he would not command them to go out into the deep." At first Jesus was only hearing one spirit speak to him, but now He was hearing all the voices of the demonic spirits inside of the man speak.

If you or I had been standing there with Jesus, we would have only seen Jesus talking at the man. Only if the Holy Spirit opened our spiritual ears would we have heard the conversation that Jesus heard.

SENSE OF SIGHT

In Eastern Europe, God was moving powerfully with deliverance, healing, and miracles in one of our meetings with the Roma Gypsy population. There was a middle-aged woman in a wheelchair, who was ushered to the front of the service to receive prayer. As I approached her, I felt an atmosphere of fear surrounding her. From past experiences, I recognized this as the spirit of fear oppressing the woman. Then in the spirit, I saw a huge demonic green snake with yellow stripes coiled around her body from the waist down. I told the men to lift her up out of the chair and have her stand as God would deliver her. As

I rebuked the demonic snake in Jesus' name, she began to suddenly and violently spin around and around in circles. The crowd saw her spinning in circles, but I saw in the spirit the snake uncoiling itself from her body. She said that she felt bones and muscles snap back into place! We all rejoiced as she was able to walk and move without the wheelchair.

SENSE OF TOUCH

A woman of God called me once to request prayer for her husband who had backslidden. She began to tell me how her home suddenly became spiritually unclean and she asked God to show her the source of what she was discerning. A few days later, as she lay with her husband in bed, she touched him. Instantly, what she described as something "slimy and gross" slid down her arm. It made her feel unclean and sick on her stomach. There was nothing physical in the room with them that could be used to explain away this occurrence. She confronted her husband about his activities and he eventually confessed that he had fallen prey to pornography and adultery. An "unclean spirit" had attached itself to his life through unclean actions. He repented, and God was able to restore him and their marriage.

IN CHURCH VS. IN GOD

One of Satan's greatest tactics is to stay hidden and influence things from behind the scenes. There is a well-known saying, "The greatest trick the devil ever pulled was convincing people that he never existed." The gift of discerning of spirits helps to pull the covers off of Satan's head. One the places that he likes to hide is within churches. One would suspect that a place of worship is the most unlikely place for a demonically influenced person to go. Luke 4:33-35 says, "In the synagogue there was a man, which had a spirit of an unclean devil, and cried out with a loud voice, saying, let us alone; what have we to do with thee, thou Jesus of Nazareth? art thou come to destroy us? I know thee who thou art; the Holy One of God. And Jesus rebuked him, saying, hold thy peace, and come out of him." The first demonic encounter recorded in Jesus' ministry was within the synagogue.

When I was 22 years old, my church hosted a weekend of fellowship with a movie night and a day of fun-filled activities. Instead of attending, I decided to stay home and seek God. The next Sunday in church, at the beginning of service, one of the men within the church interrogated me on why I wasn't in attendance for the movie night. I explained that I felt a need to spend time with God. He became upset and began to chastise me for forsaking the event. He said, "It is good to pray, but it is also good to fellowship!" He frowned upon my pursuit of God being a priority.

God began to move powerfully during the service setting people free, restoring marriages, and freeing people from emotional strongholds. The same man who confronted me was called out for needing deliverance. It was discerned that he had a spirit of anger since childhood. As deliverance was taking place, the spirit of anger began to manifest and he started to breathe heavily, frown, and growl. After the spirit was cast out of him, he sobbed and wailed for well over thirty minutes. The Friday night that I skipped movie night to pray, I had asked God to deliver people on Sunday. This man was in the church, but I was in God free! Many are in the church bound, but when you step over to being in God, you become liberated.

CONCLUSION

As you can see from reading this chapter, discerning of spirits has a great ability to allow us to see, hear, and perceive into the realm of demonic activity. Without this gift, the church loses the strategic advantage of seeing into what the enemy is doing. We never want to exalt or overemphasize demonic activity, but we want to be open to the Holy Spirit's revelations on the matter. This gift operates when God desires to bring liberty and when one is "in the Spirit!" We should never seek to peek into the demonic realm or any realm without the guidance of the Holy Spirit.

CHAPTER 4

Discerning Into the Human Spirit

HELP! I CAN'T STOP CHEATING ON MY WIFE!

Once a co-worker who I will name Kenny contacted me and asked to meet for urgent prayer. Kenny sounded anxious and emotionally heavy. A few days later, we met, and I asked him, "What's the issue?" He responded emphatically, "I have a demon of adultery! I can't stop cheating on my wife!" This young man had been in numerous adulterous affairs. Although he felt remorseful for his actions, the proclivities to "cheat" remained. To make the matter worse, he worked at the same job location as his wife and had sex with multiple women on the job.

Kenny asked me to cast out the demon of adultery that was causing him to continue in sin. As soon as I started to pray, the gift of discerning of spirits and the prophetic anointing kicked in. I discerned that there was no demon present oppressing or influencing Kenny's actions. I spoke to him, "Your issue is not a demon of adultery, but the people you hang around!" The Holy Spirit showed me that he had been hanging with a group of mostly single guys that were womanizers. I asked him, "What is this group of guys that I see around you?" He shared how he had begun to hang out with a motorcycle club and ride motorcycles with them weekly. Weekly hearing these guys boast about their sexual exploits incited ungodly desires of adultery in his heart.

The solution to Kenny's dilemma was for him to disassociate himself from the group of bikers. 1 Corinthians 15:33 (NIV) says, "Do not be misled; Bad company corrupts good character." Ungodly relationships often lead to ungodly actions. I could have stood over him rebuking the demon of adultery while yelling and screaming for it to "come out in Jesus' Name!" This action would have seemed powerful but produced no change in Kenny's life. His issue was a soulish issue resulting from wrong associations. A few years later, I saw Kenny, and he was excited to share with me how he had been faithful to his wife.

THE SPIRIT OF MAN

When we hear the phrase "discerning of spirits," most often, what comes to mind is the ability to see or perceive demonic or angelic spirits. As stated previously, these are just two of the functions of this supernatural gift of the Holy Spirit. Often, we forget that humans are spirits as well. God created humans in "his image" as three-part beings. We are a spirit that have a soul and live in a physical body. Your spirit is the real you.

Job 32:8 says, "There is a spirit in man." Our spirit is the sustaining force of our life. It is where the Holy Spirit resides within the being of born-again believers. James 2:26 says, "The body without the spirit is dead." The Apostle Paul under the inspiration of the Holy Spirit declares in 1 Corinthians 15:44, "There is a natural body, and there is a spiritual body."

One of the dimensions of discerning of spirits allows us to discern into the condition and motivation of the human spirit. There are some ministers who have propagated an unbalanced message that every problem experienced in life can be solved by casting a demon out of a person. This is untrue and has led to many wounded souls who experienced some minister yelling over them while calling out every demon, but the person walked away undelivered. While we must acknowledge the presence and activity of human spirits, oftentimes the real trouble takes its root from the condition of their spirit and soul. Deliverance ministry may be divided into two categories: deliverance from demonic activity, and inner healing from soul issues.

THE SOUL OF MAN

The spirit and soul are so closely related that they may mirror one another in their condition, motivation, and health. Proverbs 18:14 says, "The spirit of man will sustain his infirmity: but a wounded spirit who can bear?" Our souls are comprised of our mind, will, and emotions. The mind is like our central processing unit where our cognitive abilities, perception, language, intellect, and ability to reason exists. Our emotions reflect our feelings, mood, and response patterns. Researchers from the University of Berkeley California identified 26 distinct emotions that humans possess. The will of man includes one's conscience, deep convictions, and deep desires. Some individuals have been called "strong willed," meaning they are difficult to dissuade or persuade in their actions or way of thinking.

Many of us were taught as kids the saying, "Sticks and stones may break my bones, but words will never hurt me!" Derogatory, demeaning, and negative words can very well hurt a person. The damage is not seen physically, but definitely is realized internally. When these words come from parents, authority figures, or close relations, the impact on the human psyche can be severe. Many have experienced low self-esteem, a devalued self-worth, and poor self-image because of negative words spoken over them during their childhood. Mistreatment, abuse, trauma and word curses create emotional bondages within the soul that require inner healing.

"What you see is what you get!" is another adage. This saying when applied to people and personalities is untrue. There have been many accounts of friendships and marriages where one party, after many years into the relationship, exhibits characteristics and behaviors that totally shock the other parties. If you listen to the interviews of friends and family of serial killers or people that commit suicide frequently, you will hear, "I never would have imagined this person being such a way." On the surface, these people appeared "normal," but within their spirit were unresolved internal conflicts. These hidden areas of the human being may manifest when a person is under intense pressure, experience events that trigger traumatic memories, or certain stimuli in the environment are present. It takes discerning of spirits to deal with these dormant issues.

THE MAGICIAN'S MOTIVES

In Acts 8, we read about Simon the Sorcerer who enjoyed a certain prestige and power in Samaria due to the magical arts that he practiced. God sent a revival to Samaria through Philip the evangelist, where many deliverances happened, and salvations occurred (v.13), "Then Simon himself believed also." As the revival continued, the apostles Peter and John came to Samaria and many of the new converts were filled with the Holy Spirit. Acts 8:18-19 says, "And when Simon saw that through the laying on of the apostles' hand the Holy Ghost was given, he offered them money, saying, give me also this power, that on whomsoever I lay hands, he may receive the Holy Ghost."

At first glance, it seems that Simon's desire is honorable and that he is truly interested in people being blessed by God. His mouth said one thing, but discerning of spirits allowed the Apostle Peter to know his real motives. Although Simon was newly saved, he was not yet delivered from his old mindset. Simon desired the ability have the same power as the apostles so that he could restore the level of influence, manipulation, and control that he once enjoyed over the people of Samaria. Peter demonstrated this powerful gift in action as he rebuked Simon for attempting to purchase the anointing of God. Acts 8:20-23 (NIV) says, "Peter answered: 'May your money perish with you, because you thought you could buy the gift of God with money! You have no part or share in this ministry, because your heart is not right before God. Repent of this wickedness and pray to the Lord in the hope that he may forgive you for having such a thought in your heart. For I see that you are full of bitterness and captive to sin.'"

Peter discerned accurately two strongholds present in Simon's life. Firstly, Peter perceived that Simon was "captive to sin." When a person is deeply engrossed in certain sins, those same sins begin to dominate the person's mind and actions. Drug addiction is one such sin. The King James Version states that he was "in the bond of iniquity." Dictionary.com defines a bond as, "something that binds a person or persons to certain circumstances or line of behavior."

Simon was in covenant with the demonic spirits that empowered him to perform witchcraft. He was saved, but needed these ungodly bonds broken off his life. Secondly, Simon was bitter that he had lost his position of notoriety within the city. Bitterness is often a root within that causes jealousy, envy, anger, and even physical sickness. Hebrews 12:15 says, "Lest any root of bitterness springing up trouble you, and thereby many be defiled." Discerning of spirits coupled with the anointing permits us to put an axe to root issues.

DON'T MAKE ME COME TO YOU!

At a ministry conference, I once had my own Peter-like moment. I sat back as the first speaker bound up every demonic spirit from A-Z. Ahab, Jezebel, Leviathan, and every spirit in-between was called out and rebuked. As he was praying amiss, the Spirit of God came upon me and the gift of discerning of spirits went into operation. Many operate out of a book or head but fail to yield to the Holy Spirit for precise insight.

When it was my turn to speak, I boldly proclaimed, "God showed me that it is someone in this room and you are pretending to be worshipping, praising, and praying with us. This person is really here to hinder the meeting in the spirit realm and practices witchcraft." The eyes of a crowd of about 150 people widened at my declaration. A few seconds went by and no one responded to my declaration. I continued, "You are a young woman and your mother, aunts, grandmother, and uncles all have dabbled in witchcraft. Your family is from the Alabama region." Again no one responded, and the audience sat motionless in anticipation of my next action. "You are about thirty years old and the same spirits you have been serving are tormenting you in dreams," was my next statement. At this point, doubt and unbelief began to set in with the audience because no one was moving to get delivered in response to the prophetic word.

Where there is a demand or challenge, the Holy Spirit is always ready to respond. The Holy Spirit increased my discernment to know exactly where the person was seated. I forcefully decreed, "You are seated in the left section of the room and on the third row. If I have to come over to you and you don't cover up yourself for deliverance, there will be problems!" The crowd gasped in shock! Instantly, a young woman pushed her way from the third row in the left section and aggressively made her way up front to the altar. She confessed her misdeeds while weeping. As soon as I laid hands on her to break the powers of witchcraft that were operating, her body turned stiff as a board and she fell over forward. A host of demons were cast out of her, and she received Jesus as her Savior and Lord.

STEWARDING THE GIFT

The gift of discerning of spirits at times powerfully allows us to see into the lives of men, women, and children. This gift helps to protect the church from falsehood and can be used to expose sin and wrongdoing. The very nature of this gift causes it to be one that requires maturity in the life of the believer who operates in it. The gift may reveal the secrets of people's lives that could lead to embarrassment or humiliation for them if made known publicly. We must know when to speak, when to pray, when to confront, and when to keep quiet as the Holy Spirit reveals private and hidden things to us about other individuals. God's ultimate aim is the redemption of souls and reconciliation of mankind back into right standing with him.

Years ago, I attended a church service in Norfolk, VA when an out-of-town prophet was a guest speaker. As he was ministering, the crowd was wooed and awed by his prophetic gifting and preaching ability. He was full of charisma and crafty language that gained the audience's attention. While I was sitting in the audience the gift of discerning of spirits began to function as the Holy Spirit gave me insight into his life. He was quite the public performer, but God showed me privately that he operated in dishonesty, manipulated churches for money, engaged in multiple adulterous affairs, and snuck into bars to drink liquor.

After the service, the guest prophet gave me his phone number and asked me to keep in contact with him. One day, I was prompted to contact him. Surely, God would have me to reveal to him what was made known to me through the discerning of spirits and prophetic gifting. I asked the Lord, "What should I tell him first?" The Lord responded clearly and strongly, "Encourage him! He needs encouragement." I was floored. I expected God to give me a sharp word of rebuke for the corrupted minister instead God said to encourage him. Although my discernment had been accurate, God would still use the encouraging words to bring a level of repentance in his life.

Proverbs 4:23 says, "Keep thy heart with all diligence; for out of it are the issues of life." This scripture rings true when negative things are revealed to us about individuals. We must guard our heart first from being discouraged in our own walks with God. This is especially true if the gift of discerning of spirits causes us to see short-comings or character failures with those in lead-ership. Also, we must guard our heart to prevent from wrongly or prematurely judging people based on the revelations we receive about them.

CONCLUSION

Among the nine gifts of the Holy Spirit, the gift of discerning of spirits is the one that requires the greatest level of caution and stewardship. It may serve as a powerful spiritual weapon to aid in the destruction of the powers of darkness and freeing people from bondage. If improperly stew-arded, it can cause one to become imbalanced, overly judgmental, or even "spooky!" As the gift of discerning of spirits operates at an increased measure in one's life, there is a necessity that the individual equally grows in his or her love walk and being rooted in the word of God.

CHAPTER 5

Discerning the Holy Spirit

THE WATERS OF GOD

In this book, we have discussed the gift of discerning of spirits (1 Corinthians 12:10) as it relates to discerning the spirits of humans, angels, and demons. More important than these three dimensions is the ability to discern the presence, mind, and moving of the Holy Spirit. The Holy Spirit being the "third person" of the Godhead is vital to all Kingdom advancement and ministry activity. He is the most important and powerful of any spirits!

Have you ever met someone who was always discussing different demonic spirits, but clue-less about what God was doing in their midst? I have encountered many ministers who were proficient at discerning demonic spirits but were weak in discerning the move of the Holy Spirit. Exorcising demonic powers is much needed and brings deliverance. The deliverance is often short-lived if the deliverance minister does not discern how to work with the Holy Spirit to bring healing and restoration to the individual. One half of the equation is deliverance (discerning the demonic entity) and the other half is restoration (applying the work of the Holy Spirit by faith).

I sat under the leadership of a pastor who was very strong in discerning the operation of the Holy Spirit. I would be amazed as it would seem he would always know what God wanted to do next. Other ministers I know could move in the gifts (prophecy, healing, etc.), but he knew how to flow with the Holy Spirit. Once in a service, he stopped in the middle of preaching and called a lady out for being resistant to the preached word of God. She confessed that her heart was hardened because she was upset with God. Another time in service, he stopped speaking mid-sentence, left the pulpit, and ran over to minister to a lady who was secretly planning suicide. He would always just seem to know what the Holy Spirit wanted to do in a meeting.

As we grow in our relationship with the Holy Spirit, we become sensitize to His person. Our ability to discern His movement, operation, and desires increases. Also, the gift of discerning of spirits will kick in as the Holy Spirit wills. The Holy Spirit may be likened unto a stream of flowing water. When we learn to yield to Him and discern His presence, the waters continue to flow. When our hearts are closed off and not surrendered to God, those waters are held up from flowing as blessings.

Often, in a ministry setting, the Spirit of God is present hovering over the meeting place waiting for us to partner with Him in order to release a move of God. When we don't discern properly what the Holy Spirit wants to do next, this move of God may be missed.

The Holy Spirit is always active even when it doesn't seem anything is happening in the physical realm. Genesis 1:1-2 says, "In the beginning God created the heavens and the earth. And the earth was without form, and void; and darkness was upon the face of the deep. And the Spirit of God moved upon the face of the waters." If one was permitted by God to behold this creation moment, looking at the earth, it would seem nothing was happening. In the invisible realm, the Holy Spirit was hovering over the face of the waters awaiting command from God to move and create.

In our lives and in ministry, the Holy Spirit is always present. Just like the creation scenario, it may seem that nothing is happening, and life is dismal. The Holy Spirit is always waiting for us to discern His presence and instructions. His movement and manifestation are determined by our right living, faith, prayers, and words of confession. When we tap into the realm of the Holy

Spirit, the abundant life that Christ promised begins to become real in our lives.

PROPHETS AND THE GIFT

All five of the ministry graces mentioned in Ephesians 4:11 are vital to the church's growth, health, and nourishment. Each ministry grace has its own unique function that helps to strengthen the Body of Christ. In particular, two ministry graces are mentioned as foundational gifts in Ephesians 2:20, "and are built upon the foundation of the apostles and prophets, Jesus Christ himself being the chief cornerstone." These were the first two ministry graces in operation in the Early Church and Book of Acts.

In the book of Haggai, the people in Jerusalem were discouraged regarding rebuilding the Lord's Temple. God speaks to Haggai, His prophet to declare, "You have it all wrong! God says now is the time!" He properly discerned that the Spirit of God wanted them to move now to rebuild. Haggai 1:2 states, "Thus speaketh the

Lord of hosts, saying, this people say, The time is not come, the time that the Lord's house should be built." The people had voted against rebuilding, but when the prophet spoke, God's vote—will and timing—was revealed.

Prophets are known to be very discerning and having keen insight into the mind of God. Pastors and teachers may be primarily concerned about the letter of the word (logos). It is the prophets who are concerned with the Spirit of the Word (rhema). Kingdom life and church activity may become rigid, stagnant, and slowly drifting off course with the absence of strong apostolic and prophetic voices. Prophets are one vehicle that God uses to release waves of refreshing and speak the Word of the Lord to get the church back on the right path.

Prophets are powerful but should not be regarded as absolute authoritarian figures within the local church. Because the prophetic ministry is the work of the Holy Spirit operating through imperfect vessels, we must still judge and discern the accuracy of prophetic words. God gave us a safeguard in the word of God against prophets who would attempt to use their ministry for self-gain, manipulation, or self-interest. 1 Corinthians 14:29 reveals, "Let the prophets speak two or three, and let the others judge." Prophets should be graced to discern the working of the Holy Spirit which will enable them to judge if prophetic revelations from other prophetic voices are from God and accurate. This admonition provides a system of checks and balances within the prophetic ministry.

The gift of discerning of spirits may work for prophets or any believer to help us identify when a word is truly spoken from God. Regardless of the popularity or notoriety of the individual who is speaking the prophetic word to us, we must "test the spirit by the spirit" (1 John 4:1). The ability to discern if the source of a word or action is from the Holy Spirit safeguards us against getting duped, deceived, or being led astray.

APOSTLES AND THE GIFT

I believe the apostle's ministry should have the ability to discern the moving of the Holy Spirit greater than any of the other ministry graces. The governing function of the apostolic office necessitates the ability to discern the source of manifestations and the moving of the Holy Spirit. When God bestowed an apostolic mantle upon my life, the ability to discern the moving of the Holy Spirit increased. Often in our meetings, I will stop and make room for someone else to give a corporate utterance through tongues, interpretation of tongues, or prophecy. People will often ask, "How did you know that person had a word from God?" I respond, "The Holy Spirit!" Also, I would almost instantly know when someone stepped out of the timing or will of God with releasing a word or some other action within a meeting.

Apostles serve as spiritual parents ready to protect their spiritual children from threats, attacks, deception, and wolves in sheep's clothing.

Paul constantly warned the churches that he was in relationship with to beware of false prophets and false teachers. If Satan cannot get a church to fall into outright sin, then he sends in deception to bring strife, confusion, and disorder. In my own ministry, I have had to warn people about dealing with certain individuals who were mimicking the power of the Holy Spirit. In actuality, they were operating in a psychic or familiar spirit (counterfeit prophetic activity). These individuals could call out names and detailed information, but when they left the churches, disarray and chaos would always break out. In secret, these individuals operated in a lot of hidden wickedness such as astral projection and consulting familiar spirits.

A great apostle Dr. Lester Sumrall recounts in his book, "*My Story To His Glory*," how a woman approaching him said that he had a black angel while she had a white angel. He quickly discerned that not only was her words not of God but that the enemy had sent her to bring confusion. He rebuked her and said, "I have the Holy Ghost! And you have a devil." He was known for operating in the gift of discerning of spirits for deliverance and exposing demonic manifestations. Apostolic men like this were often misunderstood for their brashness, but they were often outspoken as God's guardians over the sheep and vineyard that God committed to their care.

Theatrics and sensationalism may be used to provoke an emotional response from believers. In Jeremiah 28, a prophet named Hanaiah attempted to use this tactic to wrongly influence the leaders of Judah. Jeremiah 28:2-4 says, "Thus speaketh the Lord of hosts, the God of Israel, saying; I have broken the yoke of the king of Babylon. Within two full years will I bring again into this place all the vessels of the Lord's house, that Nebuchadnezzar king of Babylon took away from this place and carried them to Babylon. And I will bring again to this place Jeconiah the son of Jehoiakim king of Judah, with all the captives of Judah, that went into Babylon, saith the Lord, for I will break the yoke of the king of Babylon." Hanaiah prophesied breakthrough and restoration. He dramatized the prophetic word (v.10) by taking the yoke from Jeremiah's act and breaking it as a prophetic sign.

Hananiah was so convincing that even the prophet Jeremiah stood in agreement. "Even the prophet Jeremiah said, Amen! The Lord do so!" Jeremiah agreed with the words of this prophet, but suddenly supernaturally, discernment kicked in within his spirit man. The Holy Spirit would not allow Jeremiah to be duped by a counterfeit prophetic word. Jeremiah exposed the folly and then pronounced God's judgment upon Hananiah for speaking falsely in the name of the Lord.

Jeremiah 28:15 says, "Then said the Prophet Jeremiah unto Hananiah the prophet, Hear now Hananiah: the Lord hath not sent thee, but thou makest this people to trust in a lie. Therefore thus saith the Lord; Behold, I will cast thee from off the face of the earth: this year thou shalt die, because thou hast taught rebellion against the Lord. So Hananiah the prophet died the same year in the seventh month."

One of the functions of the apostolic office is to prevent sensationalism and fanaticism from springing up within the church. Like Jeremiah, they are graced to expose counterfeit manifestations of the Spirit of God. Paul in his discourses cautions against false teachers, false prophets, false apostles, and wolves in sheep's clothing who emulate the external actions of true ministers of the Gospel, but inwardly are "ravenous wolves."

Apostles and prophets together are foundational to the Church. They work as a team to provide safety, protection, and purity for the Body of Christ. God graces them with an extra measure of discernment to help them function in their respective offices. When apostles and prophets are not in proper position, there is a tendency for an increase of false teachers, false prophets, and false doctrines to creep into the house of God. We need these ministry offices and the gift of discernment that they operate in to grow properly as the Body of Christ.

AZUSA STREET

The dimension of discerning of spirits that deals with perceiving the operation of the Holy Spirit was extremely strong during the Azusa Street Revival. Daily, hundreds of believers from around the world would pile into a small building on Azusa Street seeking the baptism and blessing of the Holy Spirit. Those that were present recorded how when the enemy could not stop the move of God through bad newspaper articles or persecution, he sent spiritualists to try to infiltrate the meetings. Spiritualists and those seeking attention within the meetings would stand to minister, sing, or speak in counterfeit tongues and instantly exposed. Seymour and the leaders rarely would confront these individuals directly, but in unison begin to pray for the true move of God. The Spirit of God would stop these people. Some would become confused and unable to continue in their actions. Others would fall ill or die within a short time of mocking the move of God.

The revivalist preacher, evangelist, and author Frank Bartleman writes in his book, "*How Pentecost Came to Los Angeles: As It Was In The Beginning*" stating, "Presumptuous men would sometimes come among us. Especially preachers who would try to spread themselves, in self-opinionation. But their effort was short lived. The breath would be taken from them. Their minds would wander, their brains reel. Things would turn black before their eyes. They could not go on. I never saw one get by with it in those days. They were up against God. No one cut them off. We simply prayed. The Holy Spirit did the rest. We wanted the Spirit to control."

He writes further, "The Spirit was very sensitive, tender as a dove. The Holy Spirit is symbolized as a dove. A dove has no gall bladder. We knew the moment we had grieved the Spirit, by an unkind thought or word. We seemed to live in a sea of pure divine love. The Lord fought our battles for us in those days. We committed ourselves to His judgment fully in all matters, never seeking to even defend the work or ourselves. We lived in His wonderful, immediate presence. And nothing contrary to His pure Spirit was allowed there."

The leaders during the Azusa Street Revival developed a sensitivity to perceiving the mind of the Holy Spirit and discerning His workings.

UNUSUAL MANIFESTATIONS

In our ministry, we continually witness healing, deliverance, prophecy, and the gifts in operation. Also, we encounter at times unusual manifestations of God's presence. Some of these manifestations are abnormal, intense, and unique that one has to quickly discern if they are the work of the flesh, the devil, or the Holy Spirit. The Holy Spirit will always give me reassurance when it is Him even if I don't understand in my natural mind what is taking place.

Once in a meeting, a young lady walked to the altar and motioned for the microphone as if she wanted to testify. When I handed her the microphone, she attempted to share her testimony. The most unusual thing happened. None of her words would come out in English. She could only speak in tongues. The more she tried to speak in English and stop the tongues, the stronger they became. She was so overcome by God's presence that a deep deliverance was brought to her life. At that moment, no one knew what to do but wait to see what God would do. The church laughed in joy as we all discerned it was truly the work of God.

CONCLUSION

The gift of discerning of spirits operates in seven different dimensions. They each have their own importance and role in us understanding the will of God and seeing into the realm of the Spirit. The most important of these seven dimensions is that this gift functions in is the ability to discern the mind, moving, and operation of the Holy Spirit. It is by following the leading and guidance of the Holy Spirit that we are true sons and daughters of God (Romans 8:14).

CHAPTER 6

Discerning the Kingdom Of Darkness

When Jesus appeared to me in the night vision, He corrected me concerning my teaching on discerning of spirits. I frequently taught that discerning of spirits operated within four dimensions. He shared with me that there were seven dimensions that He wanted me to teach.

He shared with me that the gift of discerning of spirits is in operation when one sees into the Kingdom of Darkness—specifically, when we are able to see and hear into the second heavens and netherworld realms.

Revelations 2:24 says, "As many as have not this doctrine, and which have not known the depths of Satan." In the Book of Revelation, Jesus appears to the apostle John and speaks about the depths of Satan. I taught earlier in this book how the gift of discerning of spirits can function to allow us to discern demonic spirits, their presence, and activity. This discernment happens at ground level warfare or what I call hand-to-hand combat. In contrast, when the depths of Satan are made known to us, we are allowed to see into the plans and activities of Satan's kingdom. These are the ruling spirits and superior demonic realms that control the ground level demonic activity.

Most Christians have never experienced seeing into Satan's kingdom. God purposely protects us from viewing the activity and wickedness that takes place in these realms. God has to prepare our hearts and mind before we can be allowed to access certain revelations. Also, He has to impart to us a divine grace to mentally handle some revelations. The appearance of some of the demonic beings in the netherworld and second heavens are so grotesque and horrifying, and thus, seeing them may open doors of fears in the hearts of men.

Before we proceed, let me issue two caveats regarding seeing into the Kingdom of Darkness.

CAVEAT 1: AVOID UNLAWFUL WARFARE

It can be dangerous to access the realms of the kingdom of darkness if one is not led by the Spirit of God to do so. Our focus in life and ministry should be to grow in the knowledge of God and intimacy with Jesus. As we pursue the Lord Himself, He may grace and commission us to engage in spiritual warfare that involves combating the "depths of Satan." Engaging spiritual powers without permission and the leading of the Holy Spirit has led many to be shipwrecked in life and ministry.

I learned this lesson the hard way. As a young believer, my faith was pumped up from watching Christian television, reading books, and spending time in church meetings. One day, in my prayer time, I began to issue challenges against spiritual powers in the kingdom of darkness. I specifically called out to battle certain high-ranking demonic powers that I had read about in books. Suddenly, the atmosphere in my bedroom changed and a sense of evil foreboding filled the room. A sharp pain shot through my side and I fell to the ground. The pain intensified as it felt like someone had my side in a vice grip and slowly turning it. I cried out to Jesus and repented for my haughty actions. The pain stopped, and I was able to get up from the ground. What I thought was faith was really ego and presumption!

There have been many books and teachings regarding spiritual warfare. The books contain great material, references, and insights. Reading a book does not give you authority to engage spiritual powers. In an effort to make money, sell books, and stay relevant, some authors have falsely taught a wonton style of spiritual warfare. Believers are taught to engage every spirit under the sun: Ahab, Jezebel, Behemoth, Python, Beelzebub, Leviathan, etc. Jesus and His apostles never taught this type of wholesale spiritual warfare.

We should be knowledgeable about things in the spirit realm, but one must be cautioned against provoking warfare unnecessarily. A person can become a target for demonic attack without God's grace to cover them. This is called unlawful warfare: spiritual warfare that God never authorized. It is likened unto painting a target on your chest and inviting the enemy to attack you without proper armor in place.

The sons of Sceva attempted unlawful spiritual warfare because they were not in right relationship with God. Acts 19:13-16 states, "Then certain of the vagabond Jews, exorcists, took upon them to call over them which had evil spirits the name of the Lord Jesus, saying, We adjure you by Jesus whom Paul preacheth. And there were seven sons of one Sceva, a Jew, and chief of the priests, which did so. And the evil spirit answered and said, Jesus I know, and Paul I know; but who are ye? And the man in whom the evil spirit was leaped on them, and overcame them, and prevailed against them, so that they fled out of that house naked and wounded."

CAVEAT 2: A LIFESTYLE OF HOLINESS

Sin creates an open door that gives the enemy access to our lives and soul. Right living and faith in Jesus Christ causes us to wear the "breastplate of righteousness" (Ephesians 6:14) that stops arrows sent from the enemy from wounding us. When we have sins of commission that we have not repented from, the enemy has an advantage against us in warfare. Anyone pursuing the deeper things of God or active in spiritual warfare must live holy. The proverbial writing, The Wisdom of Solomon 5:19 (CEB) says, "He will take up holiness as a shield that can never be beaten." Holiness creates a spiritual force-field of sorts around our being that acts as a shield.

Evangelist Angela Greening interviewed a young lady named Rebekah that she helped to deliver from serving Satan. Rebekah was part of a satanic society that was preparing her to be "the fifth bride of Satan." Her preparation included taking part in animal sacrifices, witnessing human sacrifices, and learning witchcraft. Two witches took her to a Benny Hinn crusade to teach her how to release curses. While they were attempting to curse Benny Hinn, he stopped in the middle of ministering and pointed at the three women who were afar off in the crowd of thousands. "*You three are going to hell if you don't repent! I know what you are doing!*"

In the interview, Rebekah shared how the group's demonic curses would not work against Benny Hinn. She described as "pure light" and light "like a bubble enclosed around him" that was protecting him. Also, she saw the outline of half men (men from the shoulders up) standing beside him. Later, she understood these to be his guardian angels. A lifestyle of faith and right living caused the glory of God and angels to be Benny Hinn's shield. Isaiah 58:8 (NIV) says,

"Your righteousness will go before you, and the glory of the LORD will be your rear guard."

POWERS IN THE AIR

Ephesians 6:12 says, "For we wrestle not against flesh and blood, but against principalities, against powers, against the rulers of the darkness of this world, against spiritual wickedness in high places." The demonic spirits mentioned in chapter 1 of this book attack individuals and families. The evil powers mentioned here in Ephesians 6 rule over and influence communities, regions, nations, and world systems. It takes a special ability to see into their works and realms.

There are wicked spiritual powers that operate in "high places." The Greek word epouranois also means "heavenly places." The first heaven is the earth's troposphere and stratosphere. It is the heaven that God created in Genesis 1:1, "In the beginning God created the heaven and the earth." The second heavens refer to the celestial realm that includes the mesosphere, thermosphere, exosphere, and outer space. There are fallen angels and high-ranking demons that abide in this realm. The third heaven is the abode of God and the Kingdom of Heaven. Paul says that he was caught up into the third heaven. 2 Corinthians 12:2 says, "I knew a man in Christ above fourteen years ago, (whether in the body, I cannot tell; or whether out of the body, I cannot tell: God knoweth) such an one caught up to the third heaven."

Several times, God has allowed me to discern and see into the celestial realm. In none of these instances was I seeking such an encounter. There was always some spiritual purpose involved with this type of revelation. Many times, when traveling to nations, God will allow me to see the demonic forces and ruling spirits arrayed over a territory or nation. The evil forces that I see in these situations are always more fierce and greater in influence than the ground level demonic spirits.

Years ago, my spirit was carried by the Holy Spirit into the spirit realm into the air over a region. There were hundreds of black demonic figures that resembled gargoyles that one would expect to see in Gothic architecture. Their dark-colored bodies and wings allowed them to fly in circles. There were so many of them that they appeared at times as one thick mass that blocked out sky's view. God was showing me that these were the evil powers opposing revival and prayers in this region. I wasn't afraid because the Holy Spirit was with me, but I did sense an atmosphere of pure evil. I came out of this encounter shaking and trembling.

Satan himself is called "the prince of the power of the air" (Ephesians 2:2 KJV) and "ruler of the kingdom of the air" (Ephesians 2:2 NIV). He rules over the Kingdom of Darkness, all of its realms, and subordinate demonic powers from his throne in the celestial realm. The Kingdom of the Air is the highest of Satan's realms from which global strategies for wickedness is projected into all other demonic realms. Jesus operated in the dimension of discerning of spirits that allowed Him to see into the second-heaven realm. Luke 10:18 says, "And he [Jesus] said unto them, I beheld Satan as lightning fall from heaven."

POWERS UNDER THE EARTH

There is a subterranean realm that is part of Satan's Kingdom of Darkness. This underworld or netherworld has infernal spirits that bring sickness, death, and misery to humankind. Hades and the Abyss were prepared for Satan and his angels. They both will be thrown into the Lake of Fire along with Satan and his cohorts (Revelation 20:10). Until that appointed time of judgment, Satan and his underlings operate from this netherworld kingdom as well.

Mary K. Baxter in her book, A Divine Revelation of Hell, describes how Jesus permitted her to travel into the deep regions of darkness where there was continual suffering and misery. She witnessed unbelievers and backslidden Christians who had passed away being tormented night and day without mercy. She also describes some of the strong demonic beings that she encountered in this realm who were full of wickedness. God truly gave her the gift of discerning of spirits to be able to see into the supernatural.

In A Divine Revelation of Hell, Mary K. Baxter writes concerning the demonic forces she saw in the underworld, stating, "All at once, demons of all kinds were going past us. Imps growled at us as they went by. Demon spirits of all sizes and shapes were talking to each other. Out ahead of us, a big demon was giving orders to small ones. We stopped to listen, and Jesus said, 'There is also an invisible army of evil forces that we do not see here—demons such as evil spirits of sickness.'

'Go!' the larger demon said to the smaller imps and devils. 'Do many evil things. Break up homes and destroy families. Seduce weak Christians, and mis-instruct and mislead as many as you can. You shall have your reward when you return."

Isaiah 28:14-15 says, "Wherefore hear the word of the Lord, ye scornful men, that rule this people which is in Jerusalem. Because ye have said, We have made a covenant with death, and with hell are we at agreement." There are many human servants or rather slaves of darkness that deal with these underworld powers. These are not your casual New Agers or spiritualists, but people steeped in occultism and black magic. In many third world nations, grave robbers and ritualists summon spirits of the grave and underworld demonic powers to do their bidding. When these spirits are provoked, they bring with them strong death, poverty, and bondage.

Distressed Saul consulted the Witch of Endor. Today, she would have been called The Medium of Endor or the Psychic of Endor. Saul had previously banned spiritism from the land of Israel. 1 Samuel 28:9 says, "And the woman said unto him, Behold, thou knowest what Saul hath done, how he hath cut off those that have familiar spirits, and the wizards, out of the land." Desperation caused Saul to disobey his own ordinance and consult this spiritualist. 1 Samuel 28:11 says, "Then said the woman, Whom shall I bring up unto thee? And he said, Bring me up Samuel!" Notice that the woman said "bring up" and Saul said "Bring me up!" The word "up" was being used because they were invoking the underworld.

While ministering in MadhyaPradesh, India to a crowd of thousands, God had me to call out that there was a woman in the audience who was in covenant with "spirits of death from the underworld." Also, God had me to describe one of the instruments that she used for black magic. A lady emerged from the audience and came to the front of the altar. Her face was covered with tattoos and markings that were symbolic of the covenants she had with these demonic powers. She was set free by the power of Jesus Christ from her covenant with death.

At our Dreamers Summit, a young lady shared how she had an experience where God took her into what she described as "Hell." She wasn't sure if it was a vision or outer body experience, but it felt extremely real. Through discerning of spirits, God allowed her to see into this dark dimension. When she came out of the encounter, her side was in discomfort. She checked her side and saw burn marks. It seemed this was a sign to let her know that she was not losing her mind or feigning a supernatural experience. She had really seen into the Kingdom of Darkness.

CONCLUSION

The gift of discerning of spirits may function to give a believer revelation into the works of the Kingdom of Darkness. Within the Kingdom of Darkness, there are many realms and principalities. In this chapter, only two of the demonic realms (Kingdom of the Air and Underworld) that affect mankind were discussed. The gift of discerning of spirits is one of the "mighty weapons" mentioned in 2 Corinthians 10:4 that God can use to tear down spiritual strongholds of wickedness, evil, and spiritual bondage within the Kingdom of Darkness. 2 Corinthians 10:4 says, "For the weapons of our warfare are not carnal, but mighty through God to the pulling down of strong holds."

CHAPTER 7

Discerning the Kingdom of Heaven

History records mankind's interest in contacting the spirit realm and "higher beings" who they believed held the keys to their destinies. Ancient societies including Egypt, Babylon, Greece, Sumer, and Rome all record accounts of mortals attempting to peek into the invisible realm in attempt to gain deeper knowledge, gain power, influence earthly events, or achieve supernatural god-like abilities themselves. Today, humans still desire to "know" and "see" into the invisible realm and make contact, with higher powers. The popularity of the New Age Movement is one proof of this man's desire to tap into the spirit realm.

Both humans and demonic spirits are able to access the spirit realm on earth, the astral plane on the earth and in the first heavens, and the Kingdom of Darkness in the second heavens. These realms are where spiritual warfare takes place, which affects the livelihood of men, communities, and nations. In the unseen spirit realm, angels and demons battle over the souls of men and destinies of nations. The gift of discerning of spirits can be activated in the life of a believer to see the warfare in any of these three realms (earth, first heavens, and second heavens).

LEGAL ENTRY ONLY!

Humans may access the spirit realm either legally or illegally. Legal access of the realms of the spirit happens when God and His Holy Spirit give a person permission, grace, and authority to see into the invisible realm. God provides divine grace and protection for one's physical body, soul, mind, and spirit when He allows them access into the spirit realm. Illegal access is when an individual access any dimension of the spirit realm outside of God and His Holy Spirit. Illegally or recklessly pursuing dabbling into the realms of the spirit can be dangerous with severe consequences for violators.

There are three (negative) primary ways that someone may attempt to access the spirit realm illegally. The first way is through spiritism. Spiritism is a belief that man can communicate with the spirits of the dead and beings from other dimensions. A practitioner of this doctrine may attempt to contact the spirit world directly themselves or through an intermediary. Direct contact with the spirit world may include invoking spirit beings through occultic rituals or sacrifice, astral projection, conjuring, or achieving an altered state of consciousness. Examples of contact with the spirit world through an intermediary are the use of Ouija board, tarot cards, crystal ball, or seeking insight from a medium or psychic.

The second method that one may access the spirit realm illegally is through astral projection. Astral projection is when a person's spirit-body leaves from their natural body and travels the astral plane or spirit realm. The person's physical body may be lying still in a bedroom, but their spiritual body is out conducting activities in the spirit realm. Teachings on astral projection became popular with the New Age Movement and within many eastern esoteric religions.

Astral projection is dangerous for several reasons. A person may be separated from their soul and natural body and die. Many who have had near-death experiences or undergone astral projection reported seeing an ethereal cord that connected their spirit body back to their natural body. Ecclesiastes 12 confirms this, "*Or ever the silver cord be loosed...then shall the dust return to the earth as it was: and the spirit shall return unto God who gave it.*" If this cord is severed or disconnected, the person will face an untimely and unexplainable death.

Also, astral projection is dangerous because it is done without the protection or guidance of the Holy Spirit. When a person's spirit separates from their body, the person is victim and prey to demonic spirits that can gain easy access into their souls. The spirit is not intact to act as a shield against demonic attempts to access the souls. You may astral project and see exciting things but you could return to a demon-infested body and soul. Rage, anger, lust, suicide, perversion, fear, depression, and all other challenges may present themselves after astral projection.

Lastly, some who have astral projected have encountered demonic beings that were malicious and confrontational. One man reported that his astral body was captured by some Asian men who held it prisoner and subjected it to torture. They too were astral traveling and he had to pay the price of intruding on their territory. The 14th Dalai Lama discouraged his followers from continuing one contact with a spirit named Dorje Shugden because he said the spirit was hostile and malicious. Astral projection is dangerous and should not be attempted.

The third method that one may access the spirit realm illegally is drug usage and chemical abuse. There are men and women who intentionally and purposefully use a mixture of herbs, plants, exotic berries, and other substances to make potions and elixirs. These potions and herbs are considered "magical" because they have an impact upon the partakers by inducing an altered state of consciousness that opens them up to the spirit world. There may also be some ceremony involved with the ingestion of these substances.

Revelations 9:21 speaks of eternal judgment upon those that will not repent of "their sorceries." The Greek word for *sorcery* in this verse is *pharmakeia*, which is the same root word from the word *pharmacy*. There is a thin line between medical pharmacy, sorcery, and illicit drug use. Any type of man-made substance, herb, or drug introduced into the body may affect the body's chemical balance, central nervous system (CNS), and hormone regulation. There are herbalists in Africa who have mastered the trade of herbs and potions for magical rituals, "root work," divination, and invoking of spiritual powers.

Also, certain substances are known to cross the Blood Brain Barrier. Wikipedia defines the Blood Brain Barrier as "a highly selective semi-permeable membrane barrier that separates the circulating blood from the brain and extracellular fluid in the central nervous system (CNS)." It protects the brain from neurotransmitters and hormones present in the rest of the body. Drugs such as peyote, barbiturates, mescaline, and LSD are able to cross the Blood Brain Barrier and change the neuro-chemical functioning of the body.

For example, LSD binds to serotonin receptors and produce new patterns of neuro-transmission. The God-designed chemical wall of protection blocking man's access into the spirit world is then removed and individuals may hallucinate or see visions. Many drug-abusers have reported seeing snakes, gruesome creatures, someone chasing them, or evil beings. Psychiatrists and drug-abuse counselors diagnosed them as hallucinating, but in reality, many were seeing into the realm of the spirit illegally and became victimized by demonic spirits.

For these reasons, some legal medicines may be dangerous because they cross the Blood Brain Barrier and tear down the chemical wall of defense that God designed to protect us from seeing illegally into the visible realm. Have you ever seen a television commercial for a pharmaceutical pill that will heal you of a stomach ache but the side effects may include insomnia, hallucinations, suicide thoughts, nightmare, and etc.? A former co-worker of mine once detailed how every time he took a sleeping pill, he would have nightmares and ghoulish outer body experiences. One may unintentionally open themselves up to the spirit world unnecessarily through drug usage. We should avoid illicit drugs at all cost and cautiously pray before taking high-powered legal medicines.

Whether one accesses the spirit realm intentionally or unintentionally, if it is done illegally outside of the auspices of God, then a person may be subject to demonic abuse. Satan will take the opportunity to beguile and deceive just like he did with Adam and Eve whose eyes were opened unlawfully through disobedience. Genesis 3:7 says, "And the eyes of both of them were opened."

It may seem fun, exciting, adventurous, or like a journey of self-discovery, but contacting the spirit world outside of God may have severe consequences. Some have reported emotional imbalances, nervous breakdowns, schizophrenia, having demons harass them, poltergeist activity, severe illness, seeing evil spirits, or their life falling into chaos after involvement in occult activity. Once the door of the spirit world is open, it is often difficult to close those doors. If you have engaged in any of these spiritual activities, there is deliverance through repentance, prayer, and the Blood of Jesus Christ.

SEEING THE SEA!

I have received hundreds of prophetic words spoken into my life by people all around the world. Many of these revelations are words of encouragement or confirmation. There are a few prophetic words that shine brighter than others in my memory. One of those prophetic words was spoken to me by a good friend and fellow prophet named Reggie in 2005. Prophet Reggie prophesied to me, "God is going to baptize you in the sea of glass like crystal. He will give you deep revelation of His Word and Kingdom!" I was greatly excited at the time this prophecy was released over my life, but I didn't realize it would take years, many years, before it would come to pass.

Apostle John in the Book of Revelation mentions this heavenly sea of glass. Revelations 4:6 states, "And before the throne there was a sea of glass like unto crystal." Revelation 15:2 also says, "And I saw as it were a sea of glass mingled with fire." An amazing and peculiar sight to behold! In Heaven, one may expect to see angels with wings playing the harp and riding on floating clouds. In Heaven, there are angels with wings, angels without wings, beings with four wings and four faces (Ezekiel 1), beings with four faces, full of eyes and six wings (Revelation 4). There exist sights, sounds, colors, imagery, and geography foreign to our human experience on earth.

Fast forward ten years later to the year 2015, one day, I was upstairs praying in my home. I don't recollect exactly what I was praying about, but it was just like any other time of prayer. Suddenly, in the midst of praying, the Holy Spirit caused the gift of discerning of spirits to begin functioning in me. He opened my spiritual eyes to see into the dimension of the third heaven. I saw with my spiritual eyes the sea of glass mentioned in Revelation. For moments of time, I was consumed by this fantastic vision. My spirit man remained intact, but I was able to see the sea of glass with a crystalline-like appearance and living light of various hues and colors interspersed and reflecting within and from the sea. This appearance is why the Apostle John described the sea as "crystal" and "mingled with fire."

I believe that all supernatural encounters are meant to be purposeful and bear fruit. After this heavenly vision occurred, my capacity to receive deeper revelations from God increased. Also, there was an enlarging of my ability to see prophetically into the affairs of regions and nations. The level of discernment and apostolic authority upon my life instantly increased. The gift of discerning of spirits allowed me to not only see into the heavenly dimension but receive divine impartation of spiritual graces.

THE ABODE OF GOD

The third heavens and Kingdom of Heaven are protected by a host of guardian angels and the Spirit of God. Unlike the first and second heavens, it cannot be accessed without divine permission and allowance by God Himself. It is the abode of God. Hebrews 12:22-24 says, "But ye are come unto Mount Sion, and unto the city of the living God, the heavenly Jerusalem, and to an innumerable company of angels, To the general assembly and church of the firstborn, which are written in heaven, and to God the Judge of all, and to the spirits of just men made perfect, and to Jesus the mediator of the new covenant." The "heaven of heavens" or third heavens is accessed by legal entry only.

Seers, prophets, and holy men of old at times were able to see into the third heavens. The third heaven is also called "the heaven of heavens," because it is higher than and superior to the first and second heavens. Moses speaks of the "heaven of heavens." Deuteronomy 10:14 says, "Behold, the heaven and the heaven of heavens is the LORD'S thy God, the earth also, with all that therein is." King David's account includes this term. 1 Kings 8:27 says, "But will God indeed dwell on the earth? behold, the heaven and heaven of heavens cannot contain thee; how much less this house that I have built." Nehemiah's prayer contains these words "Thou, even thou, art Lord alone; thou hast made heaven, the heaven of heavens" (Nehemiah 9:6).

Stephen was one of the biblical figures who saw into the third heavens through the gift of discerning of spirits. Acts 7:55-56 says, "But he, being full of the Holy Ghost, looked up steadfastly into heaven, and saw the glory of God, and Jesus standing on the right hand of God. And said, Behold, I see the heavens opened, and the Son of man standing on the right hand of God." The gift of discerning of spirits allowed Stephen to see a heavenly open vision. The elders and scribes that were present and persecuting him would not have seen the glory of God or Jesus because the gift of discerning of spirits was not in operation on their behalf. When this gift is in manifestation, the person that the gift is manifested in will be able to see into the realm of the spirit what others around them may not see.

When the gift of discerning of spirit is the method that the Holy Spirit uses to cause one to see into the third heavens, that person's spirit-man remains on the earthly plane, but they can see into the heavenlies. In contrast, when a person sees into heaven through being translated or a trance, their body remains on the earthly plane but their spirit is caught up with God. Paul had such an encounter. 2 Corinthians 12:2 says, "I knew a man in Christ above fourteen years ago, (whether in the body, I cannot tell; or whether out of the body, I cannot tell: God knows;) such an one caught up to the third heaven." Paul was uncertain if his experience was in the body (being transported) or outer of the body (being translated), but either way, his spirit was caught up with God.

Peter was another biblical figure that saw into the heavens through the gift of discerning of spirits. Acts 10:9-11 reveals, "Peter went up upon the housetop to pray about the sixth hour: And he became very hungry and would have eaten: but while they made ready, he fell into a trance, and saw heaven opened, and a certain vessel descending upon him." Peter didn't see God, but he was allowed to peek into the heavens and receive a divine revelation. In Stephen's account, the gift of discerning of spirits operated through an open vision. In Peter's account, the gift of discerning of spirits operated through a trance vision. Depending on the gravity of the message and level of impartation that God desires to communicate, the mode of operation for the gift of discerning of spirits may vary.

THE HEAVENS OPENED

A dear friend and accomplished minister of the Gospel shared with me a powerful personal testimony. He had traveled with some of the greatest preachers of the 70s-80s and saw many great supernatural occurrences. While in a crusade in India, his life and ministry would be forever impacted by a divine revelation. As he was listening to the evangelist minister, he was suddenly engulfed by glory of God and the gift of discerning of spirits kicked into action. His eyes were opened to see what was taking place in the spirit realm. He saw the sky crack wide open and out of the third heaven descend the Throne and glory of God. The Throne and glory appeared to consume the entire sky above the platform where the ministers gathered.

Shock and overwhelmed by the heavenly vision, my friend ran and tried to hide under a billboard on the stage. He fell to his knees to repent. Suddenly, the fear of God hit the crowd of over 200,000 gathered to hear the Gospel as they too came under a spirit of repentance. Without notice, miracles began to break out all over the crowd. The blind seeing, deaf hear, lame walking, malignant growths falling off of people's bodies, and many other such miracles happened en masse. Through the discerning of spirits, he had seen Jesus and angels appear in many meetings, but this was the first time he saw the Throne of God descend from heaven. Those in attendance received great deliverance, salvation, and blessing, but he was permitted to see what was happening behind the scenes in the spirit realm.

At Jesus' baptism at the River Jordan, the gift of discerning of spirits operated in a manner to allow him to see into the heavens. Matthew 3:16-17 says, "When He has been baptized, Jesus came up immediately from the water; and behold, the heavens were opened to Him, and He saw the Spirit of God descending like a dove and alighting upon Him. And suddenly a voice came from heaven, saying, 'This is My beloved Son, in whom I am well pleased.'" Jesus discerned the third heavens opening over His life for the outpouring of the Holy Spirit. Note that the scripture says, "The heavens were opened to Him." The scripture did not say, "*The heavens were opened to them.*" The gift of discerning of spirits caused Him to see what others around Him could not see, as to what was taking place in the heavenlies.

CONCLUSION

The gift of discerning of spirits functioning in its highest capacity allows us to see into the third heavens. What we see may vary depending on the will of God. Angels, heavenly creatures, geographic locations, the glory of God, or God Himself may be seen supernaturally when the Holy Spirit chooses. We must seek God more than an experience or revelation. As we grow close to the Lord Jesus Christ, He makes known to us the mysteries of the Kingdom of God. Isaiah 45:3 says, "And I will give thee the treasures of darkness, and hidden riches of secret places, that thou mayest know that I, the LORD, which call thee by thy name, am the God of Israel."

CHAPTER 8

Discerning the Living Word

When Jesus appeared to me in a night vision and declared that I was partially teaching the message on the gift of discerning of spirits, He declared that the gift operated in seven dimensions. Some of what has been taught in this book was spoken directly to me by the Lord. The remainder of the revelation was downloaded into my spirit. The seventh dimension revealed to me was hidden from me previously, but obviously afterward, it was made known to me by the divine revelation from the Lord. It was right there in the Word of God the entire time, but I clearly missed it.

Jesus spoke to me, "*At times when discerning of spirits is in operation, my servants will be able to discern My Word!*" This didn't make sense to me at first. I always understood that through careful study, prayer, and meditation, God would give us understanding in the Word of God. Also, anointed teachers have an ability to teach the Word and make it applicable to our daily lives. What Jesus was teaching me was that there were special instances where the Word of God could be perceived, understood, and discerned by the gift of discerning of spirits. I had never heard anyone teaching on "discerning the Word of God" or discernment in relations to the Word of God.

"Have you not read in my Word where I said that My Word was alive and spirit?" It was a rhetorical question meant to challenge my understanding but also to reveal a new truth to me.

I heard these scriptures loudly within my spirit as if the Lord Jesus was speaking to me, but He was no longer speaking to me directly. It was the Spirit of God speaking within me. John 6:63 says, "The words that I speak unto you, they are spirit, and they are life." The Word of God when spoken by God Himself, His Spirit, or in faith by an anointed believer becomes living words. The Spirit of God breathes life upon the Logos (written word) and makes it Rhema (a living word). Also, Jesus proclaims that not only is His Word alive, but it is spirit. The gift of discerning of spirits allows an individual to discern into spirits, whether a spirit being (humans, angels, demons), spirit realms (Kingdom of Heaven, Kingdom of Darkness) or the living Word which is spirit.

John 1:1 states, "In the beginning was the Word of God, and the Word was with God, and the Word was God." The Bible reveals to us in Jon 1:1 that one manifestation of Christ is as the living Word who was with God since the beginning of creation and who is God. We see the Word mentioned here not as just something one reads, but as a creative living power and spiritual force within the Godhead. John 1:3 states, "All things were made by him; and without him was not anything made that was made." The Word of God is not only alive and spirit, it also possesses creative power!

God caused past experiences and conversations that I had with individuals to replay instantly like a flash of lightning within my memory. I had been exposed to individuals including myself who at times operated in this dimension of the gift of discerning of spirits unaware. One individual that God highlighted is a woman of God who through this gifting often knows truths and insights found in the Word of God by the Spirit, having never studied them out in the Bible.

THE BOOK OF RUTH OPENS UP

Years ago, as I sat at Apostle Warren Singleton's home, he shared with me an experience that he had while studying the Word of God. One day, he opened the Bible to read the Book of Ruth. As he was reading Ruth chapter 1, the most unusual and unexpected thing happened. Suddenly, he saw what he described as "seven levels of revelations" for this one chapter that flooded his mind in a moment's notice. The Spirit of God gave him revelatory insight into the scripture through the gift of discerning of spirits without any commentary, concordance, or hard labor studying out the chapter in Ruth. As quickly as the revelations and interpretations of this one chapter was made known to him, they all suddenly disappeared.

What prompted him sharing this supernatural experience with me was a similar event that I experienced while reading the Word of God. As I was reading in the New Testament, God allowed me to see a verse in a way that I never saw it before. It was as if the fullness of the revelation from that verse was downloaded into my spirit. I remember pushing the Bible away from me and exclaiming, "My God!" Throughout the years, God had given me enlightenment in the Word of God and understanding of His teachings but this experience felt different. Never had the Word of God become so alive, real, and quickened to my inner man.

In both of our instances, we could not remember the entirety of the deep insights showed to us. For years, I wondered why God showed us these things, but we were not allowed to only comprehend and "see" them for a fleeting second. The Lord made known to me that the Word of God could be discerned by the gift of discerning of spirits. I realized that the gifting allowed us to supernaturally excavate the Scripture by the Holy Spirit operating within our spirit. This process bypassed our natural mind and short-term memory. The revelation was a direct download into our inner spirit man. God would call upon these insights over the years as needed by the Holy Spirit. John 14:26, says, "But the Comforter, which is the Holy Ghost, whom the Father will send in my name, he shall teach you all things, and bring all things to your remembrance, whatsoever I have said unto you."

THE GREAT DIVIDER!

Hebrews 4:12 states, "For the word of God is quick, and powerful, and sharper than any two-edged sword, piercing even to the dividing asunder of soul and spirit, and of the joints and marrow, and is a discerner of the thoughts and intents of the heart."

This is a very powerful verse that gives us insight into anointing that abides upon the living Word of God. This verse tells us three things about the Rhema Word: It is 1) alive, 2) powerful, and 3) sharp. Hebrews 4 compares it to a two-edged or double-edged sword. In ancient times, a double-edged sword was highly regarded by warriors because it can cut in two directions. Metaphorically, this means that the Word of God is meant to cut us for pruning, but also cut down the works of darkness. It can be an instrument of warfare or one of pruning that brings forth personal spiritual growth. Also, this analogy represents that the Word of God can produce favorable circumstances for those who obey it. In contrast, it can produce unfavorable circumstances for those who rebel against its teachings.

The Word of God is so sharp that it's "*piercing even to the dividing asunder of soul and spirit.*" Often what we call the Holy Spirit in operation or anointing is nothing more than soulish power.

The great Chinese ministry leader Watchman Nee refers to this phenomenon in his book, The Latent Power of the Soul. Many psychics, spiritualists, and New Agers have mastered soul power and masqueraded it as "anointing." This brings in familiar spirits and contamination within the Body of Christ. When the Word of God is built up in our hearts, it works in conjunction with the gift of discerning of spirits to make known if the source of an action is from the soulish or spirit realm. In addition, when the Word of God begins to dominate our inner life more than our own soul, our level of discernment heightens.

Three instances in the Book of Luke, we read about Jesus knowing the thoughts of people that challenged His ministry. In Luke 6, He knew the thoughts of those upset that He healed a man's withered hand on the Sabbath Day. In Luke 11, He knew the thoughts of those who accused Him to be possessed with the devil Beelzebub. In Luke 5, He knew the thoughts of those who were angry when He healed the paralytic and decreed that his sins were forgiven.

The divine ability that Jesus demonstrated to "know their thoughts" always intrigued and baffled me. I have known many prophets but few that were able to demonstrate this level of insight. Also, I could not find any place in the Scripture where God called us to pursue mind-readers. Nevertheless, at some point, this same ability began to operate in my own life and ministry. It would be years later after the visitation from Jesus that I would come to realize that this manifestation was the gift of discerning of spirits in operation.

While serving on the ordaining council of a pastor's consecration service, suddenly, I heard two men's thoughts. I was standing in front of the congregation prophesying to the pastor of the church, but in the spirit, I heard the thoughts of two specific pastors in the crowd. It sounded as if they were speaking to me audibly, but I heard the thoughts in the spirit realm through the discerning of spirits. The first man thought, "I'm going to ask Apostle Demontae to do the same type of ordination service for me!" The second man thought, "I'm going to set up my own consecration service where I can be elevated to an apostle as well." God revealed the first man's motivation was out of admiration. The second man's motivation was out of competition and envy.

The very next day, I shared this experience by phone with my own pastor. Literally, five minutes later, the first man whose thoughts I heard in the previous day's service called me. He sounded anxious yet excited as he posed a question. He asked, "Can you make me an apostle, or bishop or something?" I told him that God had already revealed to me that he would ask and that the answer was "NO!" God had not called him to those ministry roles and it would be outside of the will of God to ordain him as such. A few months later, I discovered that the second man set up his own ordination service and brought a ministry leader in from out of town to consecrate him to the office of apostle. The Spirit of God allowed me to hear correctly the motives and intentions of these men's hearts.

I must clarify. When the gift of discerning of spirits functions in the dimension to allow us to know the thoughts of others, it is not mind-reading. Although we may know what people are thinking, the person's spirit is being discerned not their mind. There are some thoughts that emanate from one's deep subconscious or spirit man. These are more than mere casual thoughts but are energized by deep desire and/or emotions from the person's spirit. The gift of discerning of spirits will allow one to discern these spiritually-charged thoughts. When we read of Jesus knowing the thoughts of others in the Bible, we realize these individuals' thoughts were energized with strong emotions of bitterness, resentment, hatred, jealousy, and persecution toward Jesus' ministry.

The Living Word, according to Hebrews 4:12, "is a discerner of the thoughts and intents of the heart."

MARY'S KAY'S VISION

Mary K. Baxter in her book entitled, "A Divine Revelation of Heaven," shares an account of a visionary experience given to her by the Holy Spirit:

"Once I saw a minister prophesying. As he was prophesying, God opened my eyes to see an angel over his head. The angel was pouring on him what looked like oil mingled with fire, out of a horn. Then I saw the man's heart in a vision. It was full of the Bible, the Word of God. The Word seemed to come up from his heart, into his throat, and out his mouth. I could see the Word as it came out of his mouth. As it hit the air, it seemed to become a two-edged sword.

"Another angel was recording what the man of God said. I thought, 'Oh, God, this is truly your Word going forth to the people.' Then I saw one of the angels holding the Holy Scriptures. As the man began to preach the living Word of God, the words seemed to leap off the pages of the Bible. They would go into his heart and out of his mouth. As this happened, the words of the Bible became a two-edged sword."

She further gives an account how many were healed, delivered, and set free by the power of the living Word when it was spoken. Satan, false teachers, and false prophets may all quote Scripture, but they can only share the dead letter of the Law. Remember Satan tempted Jesus in the wilderness by quoting scriptures out of context. Demons also "believe and tremble" (James 2:19). They believe the Word of God, but while in rebellion, they do not receive the truth of the Word. 2 Corinthians 3:6 says, "The letter killeth; but the spirit giveth life." Only when the Word is truly believed within the heart, received with faith, and spoken in truth does it become the living Word that is spirit and truth.

READING IS FUNDAMENTAL!

A pastor whose ministry I sat under for three years recounted a supernatural story regarding his spiritual mother. His spiritual mother was an older woman who was widowed and lived a pious life. She spent hours each day talking to Jesus in prayer and reading the Word of God. She was one of the few prophetic voices that my pastor trusted wholeheartedly.

When this woman of God was first saved, she was on fire for Jesus and spent a lot of time seeking God. Although she was fervent in spirit, there was an obstacle hindering her spiritual growth and growing in the knowledge of God. She was illiterate and thus unable to read the Bible or any other material. Life had dealt her some hard blows. She went to work as a youth and was unable to finish her formal education.

One day in prayer, she shared with the Lord how she felt inadequate being unable to read the Bible. Her spiritual life was missing a foundational element of being able to study the Word of God. God spoke to her, "Pick up your Bible and read it!" She replied, "But Lord I don't know how to read!" God retorted, "READ!" She picked up the Bible and suddenly the words literally jumped off the page. Somehow someway, she was able to read the words being illuminated by the Spirit of God.

From the day that God told her to "READ," she was able to read the Bible daily. Mysteriously, she could only read the Bible this way and no other books or literary material. The words would leap off the page each time she read as if the Word was alive. Also, this supernatural grace would only work when reading the King James

Version of the Bible. My pastor defined this occurrence as her being able to read supernaturally. Technically, she was experiencing the gift of discerning of spirits, which allowed her to discern the living Word because the Word is "spirit."

CONCLUSION

The gift of discerning of spirits, although limited in its scope to the realm of spirits, is diverse in its operation and manifestation. The most common manifestations of this gift are to discern demonic presences for deliverance, the condition of the human spirit, and the working of the Holy Spirit. However, there exist other manifestations of this gift within these three common dimensions as the Spirit wills and as God deems necessary. One should not necessarily seek these specific experiences, but we should be open to the diverse ways the Lord may desire to reveal things to us. The Word of God is alive and powerful.

CHAPTER 9

The Great Balancing Act

The gifts of the Spirit, supernatural, and prophetic ministry can be exciting and fascinating. We must caution ourselves not to be led by gifts but by the Spirit of God. The Holy Spirit gives spiritual gifts to supplement our relationship with God, and for the work of the ministry. The gifts and supernatural should never be prioritized above our desire for greater intimacy with the Lord Jesus. Romans 8:14 says, "For as many as are led by the Spirit of God, they are the sons of God." Operating in the gifts and supernatural abilities does not qualify us for spiritual sonship. Being born again through the saving grace of Jesus Christ and living in obedience to His Spirit are the marks of spiritual sonship.

Romans 11:29 says, "For the gifts and calling of God are without repentance." Spiritual gifts may be given to individuals who were once faithful, living holy, and walked with pure motives. God does not take these gifts back. Many unsuspecting believers have been wowed and wooed by a person's demonstrations of the gifts but preyed upon by these same individuals. Abuse, wounds, bondage, and even worse has occurred in many of these cases. The gifts of the Spirit (1 Corinthians 12:1-31) are powerful tools revealing the work of Christ. The fruits of the Spirit (Galatians 5:22-23) assume higher precedence in the life of believers because they reveal the nature of Christ.

Anyone called to operate in the gifts of the Spirit or flowing in the anointing should be admonished to live a life of holiness. The stronger the grace for ministry upon your life, the stronger the enemy will seek to cause you to sin. If the enemy cannot cause a person to commit a sin of commission, then he will attempt to make the individual have an imbalanced life or get off course. Submitting to righteous seasoned leaders, accountability to leadership, surrounding oneself to the counsel of proven prophetic leadership, and adhering to the Word of God creates boundaries and structure in believers' life to prevent the enemy's desires from prevailing.

Our growth in the gifts of God should coincide with our growth in spiritual fruit and character. Growing in character and our love walk will hinder pride settling into our hearts. Paul had such an abundance of revelation that God allowed a demonic spirit that stirred up persecution against him to continue in its action. 2 Corinthians 12:7 says, "And lest I should be exalted above measure through the abundance of the revelations, there was given to me a thorn in the flesh, the messenger of Satan to buffet me, lest I should be exalted above measure." Many of us that God has greatly gifted have endured wilderness seasons to prevent us from being puffed up so we can maintain a level of humility before the Lord.

"SPOOKY SPIRITUALS"

There is a tendency for individuals who are highly gifted by God or who desire to experience the supernatural to become imbalanced. This imbalance may be in their spiritual walk or personal life or both. The adage, "Don't be so heavenly minded that you are no earthly good," still rings true today. I have seen zealous believers who spent almost every waking moment prophesying, discerning demons, and discussing spiritual matters but neglecting providing for their family and own well-being. Our God is a God of order. 1 Corinthians 14:33 says, "God is not the author of confusion."

As a young believer, many things that I encountered were brand new to my Christian experience. I would meet individuals who were gifted and talked about seeing in the spirit or strange encounters they were experiencing. As a youth, I had my own share of supernatural happenings, but the frequency that many of these people reported such activity shocked me. A few times, I felt inadequate or "not spiritual enough" when I compared myself to them and the bizarre behavior some of them exhibited. A part of me began to equate being spiritually "deep" or close to Jesus with being bizarre or a weirdo.

Spiritual growth, maturity, and experience led me to a more accurate conclusion. Many of these individuals were indeed gifted and experiencing the spirit realm, but many lacked spiritual maturity. Some of the weirdness they displayed was not a result of spirituality but a result of unresolved soulish issues. Rejection, insecurity, trauma, bitterness, abandonment were just some of the soul issues that were left unhealed. When we allow the Word of God to renew our mind and the work of the Holy Spirit to transform our nature, than we stand in the image of Christ. God never called us to bizarre or weird to others who are walking in the Spirit, but He did call us to be a peculiar people. 1 Peter 2:9 says, "But ye are a chosen generation, a royal priesthood, an holy nation, a peculiar people."

We are not to be critical or judgmental of others, but God does want us to be fruit inspectors.

Luke 6:44 says, "Every tree is known by its fruit." Have you ever met someone that every conversation was overly spiritual? Have you encountered a person who is always seeing an angel? Every wind that blows or flash of light is an angel. I even knew someone who labeled anything or anyone that didn't make them feel good or rubbed them the wrong way a demon. They even tried to say that dirt in the corner was possessed by a devil that needed to be exorcised. I coined a term for these types of individuals, "Spooky Spirituals!" It may become stressful or awkward being around them because they have become ungrounded. Gifts and spiritual experiences should always produce some form of tangible fruit.

Sometimes when a person has suffered from rejection and abandonment, they try to overcompensate to gain or maintain friends. This behavior can filter over into ministry especially when you have unhealed prophetic people. I have known several prophetic people who when they stood to speak, people in the audience would smirk and glance at one another. In their minds, they were thinking, "Here he or she goes again! Another grandiose spiritual word or claim!" The discerning and seasoned believers would all know that the person was exaggerating or embellishing their revelation from God. The individual would be clueless to others who have perceived them, diminishing their own credibility, and continuing in their fabrications. The Bible warns us against such actions, "*Let no man beguile you of your reward in a voluntary humility and worshipping of angels, intruding into those things which he hath not seen, vainly puffed up by his fleshly mind.*" (Colossians 2:18).

THERE IS LIBERTY IN JESUS CHRIST

When we are truly spiritually minded like Jesus, we become a greater benefit and blessing to humanity. The mind of the Spirit of God is always focused on how to bring an abundant life, righteousness, peace, and liberty to mankind. 2 Corinthians 3:17 states, "Now the Lord is that Spirit, and where the Spirit of the Lord is, there is liberty!" The gift of discerning of spirits and the other eight gifts of the Spirit all help to bring us into freedom in Christ and fulfill our divine purposes in the earth.

Romans 8:6 — "*For to be carnally minded is death; but to be spiritually minded is life and peace.*"

Romans 10:9 — "*That if thou shalt confess with thy mouth the Lord Jesus, and shalt believe in thine heart that God hath raised him from the dead, thou shalt be saved.*"

Romans 14:17 — "*For the kingdom of God is not meat and drink; but righteousness, and peace, and joy in the Holy Ghost.*"

PRAYER

Dear Lord, I thank you for your Holy Son Jesus Christ. I thank you that you loved me so much that you gave Him as a ransom for my soul. I repent of my sins and receive forgiveness by the Blood of the Lamb Jesus Christ. By faith, I confess that Jesus is Lord and Savior. Lord, please cleanse me by your Holy Spirit and fill me with your Holy Spirit's presence. God, allow your gifts to operate in my life to bring glory to your name! Amen.

About The Author

Demontae Edmonds is affectionately known as "The Miracle Man" due to the plethora of signs, wonders, and miracles that God has performed through his ministry. He is the former pastor of Freedom in Christ Church and founder of Freedom 4 the Nations. As an apostolic ministry leader, he has traveled the globe to over twenty nations declaring the Gospel of Jesus Christ.

Throughout the United States, Europe, Asia, and Africa, he has seen the blind see, the lame walk, the deaf hear, supernatural instant weight loss, limbs grow, and many other creative miracles. As a highly sought-after prophetic voice, he has ministered to kings, CEOs, government officials, and church leaders. Pastors and leaders often gather at his meetings, and he has ministered to as many as 2500 church leaders in one ministry setting.

Demontae has been the special guest on many regional, national, and international television and radio broadcast including TBN Praise the Lord, CBN International, Turning Point, UCB Radio, Atlanta Live, Premier Radio, Power Vision TV, Oracle Television, LATENA Radio, and Cable Africa Network. Many of his short articles have been published on The Elijah List and circulated to hundreds of thousands of readers. He is proudly married to his wife Jessica and they have three beautiful kids together.

He is the author of Grab Hold of Your Miracle: 10 Keys to Experiencing Supernatural Miracles.

Get in touch with him today.

Website: www.f4nations.com
YouTube: www.youtube.com/ficmva
Contact:info@f4nations.com

Mail: Freedom 4 the Nations
Po Box 7294
Chesapeake, VA 23324

Reference

1. National Cancer Institute."NCI Dictionary of Cancer Terms."www.cancer.gov. https://www.cancer.gov/publications/dictionaries/cancer-terms/def/blood-brain-barrier (accessed August 13,2018).

Bibliography

1. Lester, Sumrall. My Story To His Glory. South Bend: LeSea Publishing, 2012. Print
2. Bartleman, Frank. Azusa Street: How Pentecost Came to Los Angeles Jawbone Digital: 2012. Print.
3. Baxter, Mary K.A Divine Revelation Of Hell. New Kensington: Whitaker House, 1993. Print.

Index

L

M

P

R

S

T

V

W

Lightning Source UK Ltd.
Milton Keynes UK
UKHW021126170519
342861UK00007B/645/P